Very Faithfully yours
Cheiro

PALMISTRY FOR ALL

CONTAINING NEW INFORMATION ON
THE STUDY OF THE HAND NEVER
BEFORE PUBLISHED

PALMISTRY FOR ALL

CONTAINING NEW INFORMATION ON THE STUDY OF THE HAND NEVER BEFORE PUBLISHED

By

CHEIRO

WITH A PREFACE TO AMERICAN READERS

AND

WITH UPWARDS OF SIXTY ILLUSTRATIONS

GYAN

Published by

Gyan Publishing House
5, Ansari Road
Daryaganj, New Delhi-110002
Phone: 011-47034999, 9811692060
E-mail: books@gyanbooks.com

Distribution Network
gyanbooks.com
India, USA, Canada, UK, Australia, France

ISBN : 978-81-212-6254-5 (PB)
First Published, 1910

2nd Impression 2022

Printed at: Gyan Press, Delhi.

PALMISTRY FOR ALL
Author: CHEIRO

PALMISTRY FOR ALL

CONTAINING NEW INFORMATION ON THE STUDY OF THE HAND NEVER BEFORE PUBLISHED

BY

CHEIRO

WITH A PREFACE TO AMERICAN READERS

AND

WITH UPWARDS OF SIXTY ILLUSTRATIONS

PREFACE

TO THE AMERICAN EDITION

THERE is no countryin the world where the "study of character" is more indulged in than in the United States of America. During my many visits there I could not help remarking how even the "hardest headed" business men used any form of this study that they could get hold of to help them in their business dealings with other men and also in endeavouring to ascertain the character of their clerks and employees.

In looking over the records of my career I find that in the course of my visits to America I gave private lessons to the heads of two hundred and seventy business establishments in New York, one hundred and thirty-five in Boston, and three hundred and forty-two in Chicago.

All these men were large employers of labour and what they principally wanted was, to have some help beyond that of their own judgment in dealing with those with whom they came in contact in the regular course of their business careers. In no other country did I find the same interest taken in the study of character from a practical standpoint.

It is for this reason that I write a special Preface for this Edition, believing as I do that my American readers will appreciate the added information I may be able to give regarding the obtaining by a mere glance at a hand a quick grasp of the leading characteristics of the persons with whom they are thrown into contact, or for whatever reason they choose to make use of this study.

Everyone knows that "the face can wear a mask," that a person may be a good actor and put on a certain expression that may deceive even the best judgment.

But hands cannot change as the result of a mere effort to please; *the character they express is the real nature of the individual*—the true character that has been formed by heredity or that has grown up with the person by long years of habit.

The characteristics alluded to below are those which may be easily observed and which are aids to a rapid judgment of character and which I have never before been able to give to the public in such a concise way.

The more elaborate details concerning the ultimate success of the person one is talking to, their more intimate character and their future development will be found in their proper place, in the subsequent chapters.

RULES FOR RAPID OBSERVATION

The Fingers

Observe the fingers. If they look short and stumpy in proportion to the rest of the palm—one may be sure that the individual to whom they belong is of an animal nature, possessing coarse instincts, devoid of real intellectuality, and belonging to the lower order of humanity.

If the fingers and the palm appear equal in length, the owner belongs to a more cultured race, He has inherited from a more intellectual line of ancestors and for all work requiring intelligence and a higher mentality he or she could be depended on, whereas the first-mentioned type could not—no matter how well he might talk or advocate his own superiority.

If the fingers look unusually long and thin, and in this way out of proportion to the palm, the man or woman will err on the side of too much ideality and refinement and is not suited to business or work requiring "level headedness" and practicality. It would be useless, for example, to put such a person in charge of work-people or over work-rooms. His ideality and refinement would be thrown away in such positions, and even with the best will in the world he would be completely out of harmony with his surroundings.

Such a man, however, could be depended upon in all positions requiring personal mental work, research, science, literature, philosophy, educational work or, in fact, anything relating to the higher qualities of the mind.

If his fingers, in addition to their length, were also knotty or jointed (joints much pronounced), he could be depended on to a still greater extent for all work requiring great thoughtfulness, detail, and concentration of mind.

If, on the other hand, these long fingers were smooth jointed, he would, while having the same desire for ideality and for everything intellectual, be impulsive and inspirational, would lack a sense of detail and a love for detail in his own work, would be visionary, artistic, emotional. Such a person would be suited to artistic work, such as painting, making designs, models, etc., but could not be trusted to perform anything requiring detail, research or science, and would be utterly useless in any position where discipline or control of others were required.

THE FINGERS CONSIDERED SEPARATELY

Let us now observe the fingers separately from the rest of the hand.

The first finger is considered as the Dictator, the Lawgiver, the finger of Ambition, the Indicator, the Pointer, etc.

If this finger is unusually long and nearly equals the second, all these tendencies are extremely pronounced.

Therefore, if your employee has this finger long, you can safely entrust him with control over, and charge of others. You will be amazed how well he or she will make rules and regulations and see that they are obeyed; but beware, Mr. Employer, lest your first finger is short in proportion as that of your employee is long, for, if such be the case, you too will have "to toe the line" and you may find yourself in a very disagreeable position.

But let me give you a further warning: Should this man or woman have a first finger that is long and crooked, you will assuredly find out to your cost that the personal ambitions of such an individual are "crooked." Such an employee would be perfectly unscrupulous in finding out your secrets and getting you into his power.

If the second finger is straight and well shaped, its owner will be very serious, a little inclined to melancholy, but will pay due regard to whatever responsibilities with which he may be entrusted, but again beware if this finger is crooked. In this case the owner would be, however, more subject to what may be called "a crooked fate" than wilfully "wrong." Such people are, as a rule, the children of strange circumstances over which they seem to have no control. They are continually getting themselves into trouble and into false positions, but, I must admit, more by a strange fatality of things than by their own wilful actions. Nevertheless, such infelicities might be very unpleasant for their employer, especially if he has more heart than brains.

The third finger, if extremely long and straight, indicates an extraordinary desire for glory, celebrity, publicity and the like; and although this might be an extremely good quality in the case of an actor, preacher, politician or public man, it may be most undesirable if such a person is to occupy the position of a private secretary, or the confidential clerk to some family lawyer.

If this finger is crooked as well as very long, all the above qualities will be intensified and exaggerated. The love of spending money and fondness for show will also be more marked, the gambling tendencies very pronounced. No position involving the handling of money, should be entrusted to the possessor of such a finger.

The fourth, or little finger, if long (passing the nail joint of the third) is indicative of power of speech and subtlety in choice of language—the saying "to twist a person round one's little finger" originated from this very sign. Such people have a marvellous gift of speech, eloquence and flow of language, valuable gifts, of course, for orators and public persons, but not desirable qualities in a wife if a man is fond of sleep.

A short "little finger" denotes the reverse of the above. Such persons find the greatest difficulty in expressing what they want to say, but they can write better than speak and should be encouraged to do so.

These individuals have, however, not much power over others and the shorter the "little finger" is, the more timid and sensitive they are in the presence of strangers. If this finger is crooked, then these weaknesses are all the more emphasised, but if formed *crooked and long* the power of eloquence is also crooked. Such people will tell any "fairy tale" to suit their purpose—they are natural born liars and the position of President of the Ananias Club is their rightful inheritance.

The first and third fingers absolutely of equal length is the best sign of *an equally balanced mind*, but such a sign is rather rare to find.

When the fingers are very supple in the joints and turn backwards or outwards from the palm, it is an indication of a quick wit and clever brain; but such persons lack continuity of purpose. They have no "hold," as it were, on any one thing.

Fingers slightly curved inwards towards the palm, denote persons slow to grasp an idea, or a subject, but such people have retentive memories and "hold" or grip, as it were, any one thing they may take up.

CHARACTER SHOWN BY THE THUMB

The thumb is in itself more expressive of character than any other member of the hand. It was d'Arpentigny who wrote "the thumb individualises the man."

Medical science has proved that there is such a thing as a "thumb centre" in the brain and any pressure or disease in that part of the brain *shows its effect in the thumb.*

A large well-made thumb is the outward and visible sign of a strong-willed, determined person, be he man or woman.

The longer the thumb, the more the power of will rules the actions; the shorter the thumb, the more brute force and obstinacy sways the nature.

The shorter and more thick-set the nail phalange is, giving the appearance of a club, the more ungovernable is the person in his or her temper. Such people have no control over themselves and under the least opposition will fly into a blind rage of fury. This curious formation has been called the "Murderer's Thumb" because so many who have committed murder in a mad fit of passion have been found with this curious formation.

An employee with this class of thumb should never be given any position of authority over others, for he could not curb his ungovernable temper. He would also be absolutely unbalanced in his jealousy, and no woman who has the ambition to live to the usual "threescore-years-and-ten" should risk marriage to a man with one of these thumbs. But as "love is blind" it is useless, I know, to give advice in such a case.

The first joint or nail phalange of the thumb, when long and thin, denotes the opposite of the above characteristics. In such cases the person has the most absolute control over his temper, his will power is also strong but quick and unobtrusive, and in a firm, determined way people with such a thumb manage others and bend those around them to their purpose.

The second joint, if delicately shaped, almost "waist like," indicates tact, diplomacy, and gentleness, also subtlety in argument; but if this part of the thumb be full-looking or equal in size to that of the nail phalange, it denotes the person who cares nothing for tact but who, on all occasions, will speak his mind plainly, and with brutal frankness.

When the thumb looks as if it were "tied in" close to the hand, the person is timid, easily frightened by both people and circumstances, narrow-minded in his views, and miserly in his habits. It is a well-established fact that the thumbs of all misers are "tied in" and cramped-looking. It is perhaps this very fear of things and people that in the end makes them misers with their gold.

One need never waste one's time asking a person with one of these cramped-looking thumbs to do a favour, and may God help the business man or woman who ever gets into such a person's clutches!

A thumb with the nail joint supple (bending backwards or as it is also called "double jointed") indicates a character the exact opposite of that associated with the "tied in" thumb. Possessors of such a thumb are generous, adaptable to others, extravagant, and impetuous in their actions and decisions. They promise things quickly and are more often heard to say "Yes" than "No"; but if they have time for reflection, they very often go back on their promises.

Individuals having a "stiff-jointed" thumb, on the contrary, cannot easily adapt themselves to others. They are distant and more reserved with strangers. When asked to do a thing, they generally first say "No," but on reflection or when reasoned with, they often give in to the other and generally regret having done so. It is useless to oppose such people—if one cannot lead them, it is no use attempting to force them against their will.

This type has more self-control than the type of people with the "supple jointed" formation, and is not so generous or extravagant. Individuals of this group, however, make more reliable friends, so their friendship, though difficult to obtain, is generally worth having.

A thumb standing very far out from the hand (almost at right angles to the palm) is not a good sign for ordinary success. Such people go to extremes in everything they do and are generally fanatics in religion, social reform, or whatever line of thought occupies their attention.

HANDS, HARD AND SOFT

Even in the simple act of shaking hands, one can form conclusions about character.

Beware of any man or woman whose hand seems to slip from yours when you grasp theirs in greeting. Such persons are deceptive and treacherous. They may smile at you with their lips, but instinctively they regard you as their prey and will only use you for their own object.

A soft, fat hand is the indication of an indolent and more or less lazy person.

A firm hand is the sign of an energetic, reliable nature.

A very thin hand denotes a restless energetic disposition, but one that is given to worry, and fretting and is generally discontented.

A thin hand that feels listless in one's grasp denotes a weak constitution that has only sufficient energy to live.

A cold, clammy hand is also a sign of poor health, but generally that of a very sensitive and nervous person.

A person who keeps his hands closed while talking, is distrustful in his nature, has little self-reliance and can seldom be relied on by others.

A man or woman who gives a good firm grasp of the hand, is self-confident, energetic, and generally reliable.

When all the fingers (especially if the fingers be long) are seen always clinging, sticking, as it were, or folding over one another it denotes very doubtful qualities in the nature of their possessor and a decided tendency towards thieving and general lack of moral principal.

Remember that the hands *are the immediate servants or instruments of the brain.* There are more motive and sensory nerves from the brain to the hand than to any other portion of the body and, whether sleeping or waking, they continually and unconsciously reflect the thought and character of the mind or soul of the individual.

It will, then, be seen from these observations that without looking at the lines of the hand, one may be able to obtain certain details of character that are more trustworthy than those given by the face, and that these rules, if followed, should be of the greatest assistance and value to people in all walks of life.

Many of these observations are further amplified

in subsequent chapters of this work. There is not a single one of these rules that has not been proved by me in my long professional career, and knowing that they will bear the strictest inquiry and observation, it gives me pleasure now to offer them to the readers of the American Edition of *Palmistry for All.*

CHEIRO.

LONDON, March, 1916.

INTRODUCTION

IT was on July 21, 1894, that I had the honour of meeting Lord Kitchener and getting the autographed impression of his right hand, which I now publish for the first time as frontispiece to this volume. The day I had this interview, Lord Kitchener, or, as he was then, Major-General Kitchener, was at the War Office, and to take this impression I had to use the paper on his table, and, strangely enough, the imprint of the War Office may be seen at the top of the second finger—in itself perhaps a premonition that he would one day be the controlling force of that great department.

Lord Kitchener was at that moment Sirdar of the Egyptian Army. He had returned to England to tender his resignation on account of some hostile criticism about "the Abbas affair," and so I took the opportunity of his being in England to ask him to allow me to add his hand to my collection, which even then included some of the most famous men and women of the day.

As Mr. T. P. O'Connor, in writing recently of Lord Kitchener, said: "One of his greatest qualities, at once useful and charming, is his accessibility. Anybody who has anything to say to him can approach him; anybody who has anything to teach him will find a ready and grateful learner."

My experience can indeed bear out the truth of this clear judgment of one of the leading traits in Lord Kitchener's character. That very year, 1894, was a notable one in his life; his strong-willed action over the Abbas affair was completely vindicated; he was made a K.C.M.G., and returned to Egypt with more power than ever.

Once in his presence he put me completely at my ease, and in a few moments he appeared to be deeply interested in observing the difference between the lines in his own clearly-marked palm and those in dozens of other impressions that I put before him.

He was then almost forty-four years of age, and I remember well how I explained the still higher positions and responsibilities that his path of Destiny mapped out before him. The heaviest and greatest of all would, I told him, be undertaken in his sixty-fourth year (1914), but how little either of us thought then that in that year the most terrible war of the century would have broken out.

Believing, as I do, in the Law of Periodicity playing as great a rôle in the lives of individuals as it does in nations, it is strange to notice that the same radix numbers that governed Lord Kitchener's career when he was planning out the Egyptian campaign, which resulted in his great victories of Atbara and Omdurman in 1896 and 1897, are exactly the same for him in 1914–1915, and 1916 gives again the same radix number that in 1898 saw him receive a vote of thanks from both Houses of Parliament, and a gift of £30,000 from the State.

From the standpoint of those interested in this strange study of hands, the accompanying impression of Lord Kitchener's cannot help but be regarded as of great importance. In it, the rules of Palmistry that I have given in the following pages are borne out in all their details.

Returning to the impression of this remarkable hand; even in shape alone one may read by the rules of this science the following clearly-marked characteristics:

Length of fingers—intellectuality (page 134), strong determination and will-power (chapter on the Thumb, page 127), mentality and firm determination of purpose (*see* Line of Head, page 17).

The remarkable Line of Fate running up the centre of the hand and turning towards the first finger, denotes ambition and domination over others (page 52).

The Line of Success and Fame, starting on the hand from the Line of Life and ascending to the base of the third finger, exactly coincides with the period in Lord Kitchener's career when he began to find recognition and success (page 63).

As in my larger work on this subject I published Gladstone's hand as a remarkable illustration of the truth that may be found in this study, so in this present work with the same confidence I give this illustration of Lord Kitchener's as another proof of character indicated in the shape and lines of the hand, and as it has been said so often that "Character is Destiny," so it is surely not illogical to point out that in following the rules laid down by this study one may obtain a clear idea of the destiny that the Character, Will, and Individuality trace out in advance—tracks, as it were, stretching far out into the distant future for the engine of purpose and achievement to find already laid and ready to be used at the "appointed time."

In conclusion, as I have now completely retired from all professional work, I may be allowed to point out that I am not publishing this book with the idea of seeking clients. I have no desire but to see this strange study taken up as a useful and practical means of obtaining an exact judgment of the character, qualities, and hidden tendencies that might otherwise be ignored.

I think that if all parents knew at least something of Palmistry, the vast majority of children would be more usefully trained and their proper tendencies developed.

It is often too late when a child discovers—and most probably by accident—some tendency or talent that had never been suspected by its parents.

It is no wonder that so few persons find their true vocations in the world, when it is remembered the random, haphazard way in which children are brought up—educated for the most part in some scholastic mill that grinds down all to the same dead level of mediocrity, and then turns them into the Army, the Church, or into trade.

If, on the contrary, all these studies that teach the understanding of character were more encouraged, parents would have less excuse for the supreme ignorance they now show as to the real nature of those children who hold them responsible for their entry into the battlefield of existence.

These same parents would lift up their voices in righteous indignation if soldiers were sent into battle untrained, without their proper equipment, and yet these same parents have never, in the whole course of their lives, made the simplest study of any one of those many subjects by which they could in knowing the nature of their child, have strengthened weak points in the fortress of character, or by developing some talent or gift, doubly armed him for his entry into the battle of life.

It is from this standpoint that I earnestly hope this study of hands may some day be taken up. It was from this standpoint that I interested such men as Gladstone, Professor Max Müller, of Oxford, Lord Russell, when he was Lord Chief Justice, King Edward VII., and many others too numerous to mention; and lastly, it is from the same standpoint that I have now written this book, which under the title of *Palmistry for All*, will, I hope, appeal to all classes, and cause such an interest in the Study of Character that, instead of such an art being left in the hands of a few, it will, on the contrary, become universally used for the benefit of all.

CHEIRO.

NOTE.—Cheiro retired from all professional work some time ago, and the public is therefore warned against persons pretending that they are the real "Cheiro," and endeavouring to pass themselves off as the author of his well-known works.

CONTENTS

PART I

PALMISTRY OR CHEIROMANCY

Contents

ILLUSTRATIONS

CHEIROGNOMY

ILLUSTRATIONS

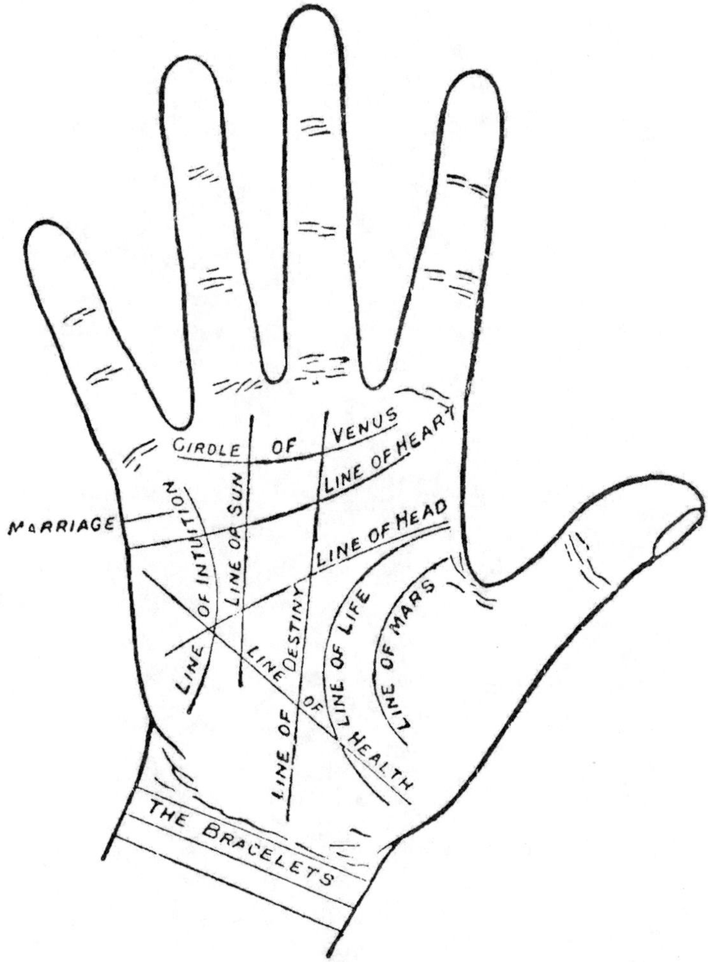

THE LINES OF THE HAND.

Palmistry for All

PART I—PALMISTRY OR CHEIROMANCY

CHAPTER I

A BRIEF RÉSUMÉ OF THE HISTORY OF THE STUDY OF HANDS THROUGH THE CENTURIES TO THE PRESENT DAY

THE success I had during the twenty-five years in which I was connected with this study was, I believe, chiefly owing to the fact that although my principal study was the lines and formation of hands, yet I did not confine myself alone to that particular page in the book of Nature. I endeavoured to study every phase of thought that can throw light on human life; consequently the very ridges of the skin, the hair found on the hands, all were used as a detective would use a clue to accumulate evidence. I found people were sceptical of such a study only because they had not the subject presented to them in a logical manner.

There are hundreds of facts connected with the hand that people have rarely, if ever, heard of, and I think it will not be out of place if I touch on them here. For instance, in regard to what are known as the corpuscles, Meissner, in 1853, proved that these little molecular substances were distributed in a peculiar manner in the hand itself. He found that in the tips of the fingers they were 108 to the square line, with 400 papillæ; that they gave forth certain distinct crepitations, or vibrations, and that in the red lines of the hand they were most numerous and, strange to say, were found in straight individual rows in the lines of the palm. Experiments were made as to these vibrations, and it was proved that, after a little study, one could distinctly detect and recognise the crepitations *in relation to each individual*. They increased or decreased in every phase of health, thought, or excitement, and were extinct the moment death had mastered its victim. About twenty years later, experiments were made with a man in Paris, who had an abnormally acute sense of sound (Nature's compensation for want of sight, as he had been born blind). In a very short time this man could detect the slightest change or irregularity in these crepitations, and through the changes was able to tell with wonderful accuracy about how old a person was, and how near they were to illness, and even death.

The study of these corpuscles was also taken up by Sir Charles Bell, who, in 1874, demonstrated that each corpuscle contained the end of a nerve fibre, and was in immediate connection with the brain. This great specialist also demonstrated that every portion of the brain was in touch with the nerves of the hand and more particularly with the corpuscles found in the tips of the fingers and the lines of the hand.

The detection of criminals by taking impressions

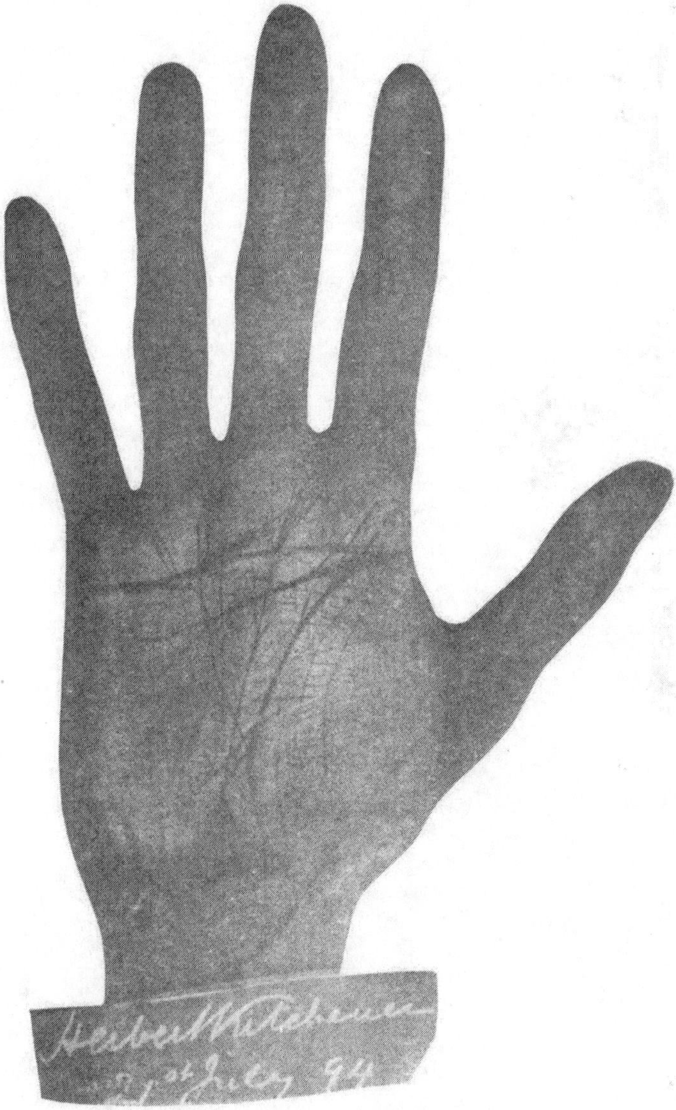

LORD KITCHENER'S HAND.

of the tips of the fingers and by thumb marks is now used by the police of almost every country, and thousands of criminals have been tracked down and identified by this means.

To-day, at Scotland Yard, is to be seen almost an entire library now devoted to books on this side of the subject and to the collections that the police have made, and yet, in my short time, I remember how the idea was scoffed at when Monsieur Bertillon and the French police first commenced the detection of criminals by this method. If the ignorant prejudice against a complete study of the hand were overcome, the police would be greatly assisted by studying the lines of the palm, and acquiring a knowledge of what these lines mean, especially as regards mentality and the inclination of the brain in one direction or another.

It is a well-known fact that, even if the skin be burned off the hands or removed by an acid, in a short time the lines will reappear exactly as they were before, and the same happens to the ridges or "spirals" in the skin of the inside tips of the fingers and thumb.

The scientific use of such a study could also be made invaluable in foreseeing tendencies towards insanity, etc.

Sir Thomas Browne, in his *Religio Medici*, after referring to Physiognomy, says:

"Now there are besides these characters in our faces certain mystical figures in our hands, which I dare not call mere dashes, strokes *à la volée* or at random, because delineated by a pencil that never works in vain, and hereof I take more particular notice because I carry that in mine own hand which I could never read nor discover in another."

But prejudice is a hard thing to combat, and, in consequence, a study which could render untold aid to humanity has been neglected in modern times. Yet it cannot be denied that this strange study was practised and followed by some of the greatest teachers and students of other civilisations.

Whether or no these ancient philosophers were more enlightened than we are has long been a question of dispute, but the one point and the most important one which has been admitted is, that in those days the greatest study of mankind was man. It is, therefore, reasonable to suppose that their conclusions are more likely to be correct than those of an age like our own—famous chiefly for its implements of destruction, its warships, its dynamite, and its cannon.

This study of hands can be traced back to the very earliest, most enlightened forms of civilisation. It has been practised by the greatest minds in all those civilisations, minds that have left their mental philosophies and their monuments for us to marvel at. India, China, Persia, Egypt, Rome—all in their study of mankind have placed the greatest store in their study of the hand.

During my stay in India, I was permitted by some Brahmans (descendants of the Joshi Caste, famous from time immemorial for their knowledge in occult subjects) with whom it was my good fortune to become intimately acquainted, to examine and make extracts from an extraordinary book on this subject which they regarded as almost sacred, and which belonged to the great past of the now despised Hindustan.

As the wisdom of the Hindus spread far and wide across the earth, so the theories and ideas about this study spread and were practised in other countries. Similar to the way in which religion suits itself to the conditions of the country in which it is propagated, so has it divided itself into various systems. It is, however, to the days of the Greek civilisation that we owe the present clear and lucid form of the study. The Greek civilisation has, in many ways, been considered the highest and most intellectual in the world, and here it is that Palmistry or Cheiromancy (from the Greek χείρ, the hand) grew and found favour in the eyes of those who have given us laws and philosophies that we employ to-day and whose works are taught in all our leading colleges and schools.

It is a well-known and undisputed fact that the philosopher Anaxagoras not only taught but practised this study. We also find that Hispanus discovered on an altar dedicated to Hermes a book on Cheiromancy, written in gold letters, which he sent as a present to Alexander the Great, as "a study worthy of the attention of an elevated and enquiring mind." Instead of it being followed by the "weak-minded," we find, on the contrary, that it numbered amongst its disciples such men of learning as Aristotle, Pliny, Paracelsus, Cardamis, Albertus Magnus, the Emperor Augustus, and many others of note.

This brings us down to the period when the power of the Church was beginning to be felt outside the domain and jurisdiction of religion. It is said that the early Fathers were jealous of the influence of this old-world science. Whether this be true or not, we find that it was bitterly denounced and persecuted by the early Church. It has always been, that the history of any dominant creed or sect is the history of opposition to knowledge, unless that knowledge come through it. This study, therefore, the offspring of "pagans and heathens," was not even given a trial. It was denounced as sorcery and witchcraft; the devil was conjured up as the father of all such students, and the result was that through this bitter persecution, the study was outlawed, and fell into the hands of vagrants, tramps, and gipsies. In spite of this persecution it is interesting and significant to notice that almost the first book ever printed was a work on Palmistry, *Die Kunst Ciromantia*, printed in Augsburg, in the year 1475.

In examining this subject it will be found that in the study of mankind it came to be recognised that, as there was a natural position on the face for the nose, eyes, lips, etc., so also on the hand was there a natural position for what is known as the Line of Head, Line of Life, and so on. If these were found in some unnatural position they would equally be the indications of unnatural tendencies. It doubtless took years of study to name these lines and marks, but it must be remembered that this curious study is more ancient than any other in the world.

In the original Hebrew of the Book of Job (chap xxxvii., ver. 7), we find these significant words: "Goc caused signs or seals on the hands of all the sons o men, that the sons of men might know their works.'

As the student of anatomy can build up the entir system from the examination of a single bone, so ma a person by a careful study of an important membe of the body such as the hand, apart from anythin superstitious or even mystical, build up the entir action of the system and trace every effect back t its cause.

To-day the science of the present is coming to th

rescue of the so-called superstition of the past. All over the world scientists are little by little sweeping aside prejudice and beginning to study occult questions. Perhaps the "whys and wherefores" of such things may one of these days be as easily explained as are those wireless waves of electricity that carry messages from land to land.

CHAPTER II

THE LINE OF HEAD OR THE INDICATIONS OF THE MENTALITY

THE object of the following chapters is to give clear and unmistakable instruction on the lines and markings of the hands, both from the student's standpoint and from that of the general reader. This is not usually the course adopted in books printed on this subject which have to appeal to a general public.

During my twenty-five years' professional experience in England, America, and other countries, I have carefully noted down the questions that are not answered in books published on this subject. I have also recorded what are the difficulties that arise in the minds of those students who meet this, that, or the other mark or line and search in vain for some explanation as to its meanings. I may add that there is not a single point on which I give information that has not been proved by me from probably thousands of cases that have come before me during my own professional experience.

As regards illustrations, I have endeavoured to make these of the simplest and clearest kind possible. I have every confidence that if they are carefully studied, no student can fail to grasp this subject in a masterful manner, and that whoever acts upon the advice I give in these pages, cannot fail to become successful as an interpreter of this study.

In all my work I regard the Line of Head (page 11) or the Line of Mentality as the most important sign that can be found in the hand.

A Line of Head is like the needle in the compass, without a true knowledge of which it is impossible to grasp the "direction of the subject." I have seen more mistakes caused by a lack of grasp of this point than by anything else.

I have seen, for example, many students make the mistake of paying great attention to what looked like a good Line of Sun or Success, and, at the same time, not noticing a weak, badly formed Line of Head, which contradicted the promise of success given by the various lines. If, on the other hand, the student had first noticed the Line of Head, he would have been able to tell the subject that the promise of success was not backed up by the intelligence or the mentality.

As regards the future being foreshadowed, it has been demonstrated that the brain is always growing, changing, increasing, or diminishing. These changes commence years before the effect is shown by the thoughts or actions of the individual. A boy ten years old may at that point commence a development which will not be felt until he is thirty, and then it may change his whole life and career. As this development commences at ten, even at that age it has affected certain nerves, and they in their turn have already affected the Line of Head—a full twenty years before the point of change or action has been reached. It therefore follows that the future may be seen and told by a careful examination of the hand which, as Aristotle has said, is the "organ of all organs, the active agent of the passive powers of the entire system."

THE LINE OF HEAD AND ITS VARIATIONS

The Line of Head (page 11), or indication of the Mentality of the subject, must in all cases be considered as the most important line on the hand. The greatest attention should be paid to it, so as to obtain a clear grasp of the Mentality under consideration.

The two hands must be carefully compared—the left showing the inherited tendencies, the right the dveloped or cultivated qualities. The slightest change or deviation in the markings from the left to the right should be carefully noted down or remembered.

The direction or the termination or end of the line should, above all, be distinctly noted, for the all-important reason that this shows the direction that the Mentality is inclined to develop towards. For example, if found with the end of the line sloping downwards in the left hand, and having become straight or lying across the palm in the right—the student is safe in concluding that the subject has not been able to follow his natural bent, but by the force of circumstances has been obliged to make himself more practical, to study business methods, and to have undertaken a training towards practicality and level-headedness in order to rise equal to the circumstances that he found himself forced to meet.

In this way the student obtains an insight into the earlier conditions of the life under examination that is invaluable, especially when there is, as will be found in many cases, no Line of Destiny visible in the early years.

If, on the contrary, the Line of Head is found

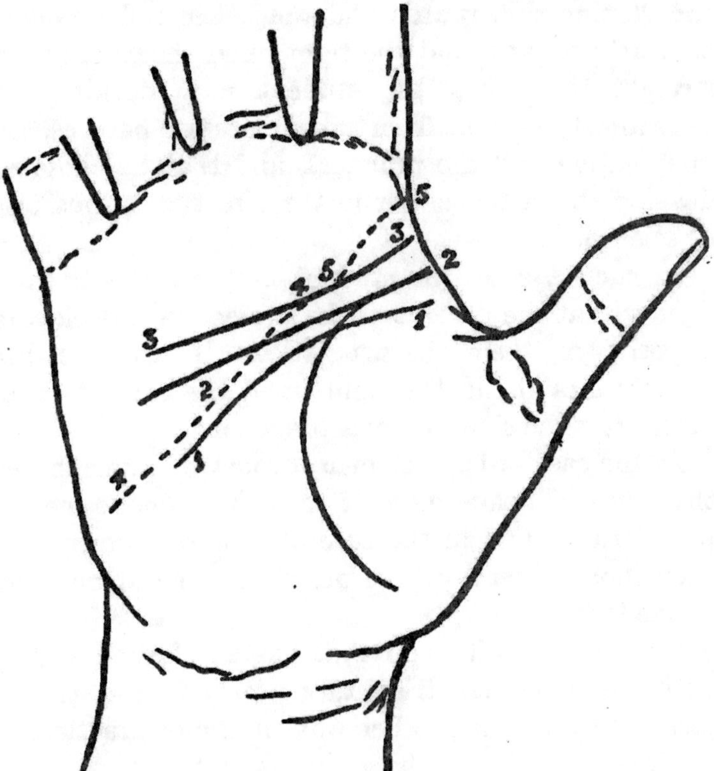

PLATE I.

THE THREE PRINCIPAL POSITIONS FOR THE COMMENCEMENT OF THE LINE OF HEAD.

exactly in the same position on the right hand as on the left, or even very nearly so, the student can be sure that there was little or no strain in the early years, but that the subject had easy conditions which were favourable, and which allowed him to develop his natural bent of Mentality.

If, however, it is found that the left hand shows a forked ending to the Line of Head, namely, one end sloping downwards and the other end straight, or nearly so, and that the right hand shows only the straight line, then the student may decide that the subject inherited from the parents two natures, the imaginative and the practical, and that he chose to develop the latter, either in the direction of business or science.

In such a case, the student may state with confidence that the parents of the subject were decidedly opposite in their characteristics. If the line has become straight in the right hand the subject takes more after the side that was practical.

In the case of boys or men it must be remembered that they will take more after their mother's mental peculiarities, and in the case of girls or women that they more generally take after the mental qualities of the father.

On a man's left hand that has the forked ending with the upper end straight, or nearly so, the student can state that the mother was the more practical of the parents. If on the right hand the same mark has become clearest the man developed, followed, or cultivated the mental qualities of the mother more than those of the father. When reading a woman's hand the reverse will apply.

If, on the contrary, the lower line was the more developed on the right hand, then the subject, if a man, had developed the imaginative or artistic qualities of the mother, and *vice versa* if the subject be a girl or a woman.

When the Line of Head looks light or faint on the left, and strong and clear on the right, the student can safely state that the subject did not inherit any strong mental bent from either parent, but has cultivated and developed his own mentality.

In such a case the subject has been a hard mental student, and has become mentally superior to his or her parents. This is often found in the case of "self-made" men or women, who have had little or no education in their early life or in their home, but who from an innate love of education developed themselves mentally. Such a sign would speak volumes for the will power and ambition of the subject under examination.

If the Line of Head is lighter and poorer on the right hand than on the left, the student can state that the subject has not made the most of his opportunities mentally, and that he has not, and never will, equal the brain power and education of his or her parents.

In such a case one may also be sure that the subject has not a very strong will power—at least mentally—although he might be very obstinate by nature, which will be seen from the quality exhibited by the nail phalange of the thumb (page 129).

A poor or non-developed Line of Head in the right hand of any man or woman is also the indication of a lack of purpose or ambition—there being no ambition where a want of mental desire and development is so distinctly shown.

A clean cut deep Line of Head is a more powerful sign of mentality than when the line is very broad, or lying, as it were, merely on the surface of the palm.

A wide broad line shows less concentration and a

more vacillating changeable nature. This rule applies with equal truth to all the lines on the palm.

Broad, coarse-looking lines are more a constitutional sign than a mental indication. They are often found in cases where the subject leads a robust outdoor life, and those who have developed the physical side of their nature more than the mental.

Great brain workers usually have thin, fine, clean-looking lines, and especially that of the Line of Head.

It will thus be seen that by observation the student will be enabled to class the sort of life led by the person under examination. No matter how intellectual a man or woman may look, the lines on the hand will indicate whether or not they have developed their intellectuality. In this way it will be seen that a study of the hand becomes a far more accurate guide than the study of the face. Many men and women may have handsome, intellectual faces and yet prefer sport or outdoor life to any mental pursuit or exercise.

Turning from an examination of the direction or ending of the Line of Head, the student must next examine the indications of the beginnings of this important Line. For example, the Line of Head may commence in three distinct different ways.

(1) From inside the Line of Life (1–1, PlateI.).
(2) Joined to the Line of Life (2–2, Plate I.).
(3) And outside the Line of Life (3–3, Plate I.).

The first is the most uncertain of all. It denotes an over-sensitive, over-cautious, timid person. It also indicates a highly nervous, easily excited individual, one who has little control over himself or his temper, who is easily put out over trifles, and liable to do the most erratic things, or fly off at a tangent when irritated. Such people are always in trouble, generally fighting or quarrelling with those about them and over things that are of no consequence. They are likewise so easily wounded in their feelings, that even a look or an imagined slight will put them out of humour or upset them for days.

If this Line of Head farther out in the palm become straight, it denotes that the subject will, later, by the development of his intelligence largely overcome this failing of over-sensitiveness. If the line slope much or bend down towards the wrist or on to the Mount of Luna (the Mount of Imagination), then the subject will become still worse with his advancing years. If the Line of Head is also poorly marked, or with "hair lines" from it, it is often the indication of some form of insanity which is likely to cause the subject to be placed under restraint in later life.

If, with this latter indication, the student also finds all the upward main lines, such as the Line of Destiny, etc., fading out past the middle of the palm, the indication of insanity and restraint becomes all the more certain.

This class of Head Line is largely found in cases where the subject is naturally inclined towards drink and intemperance of every description.

Even in cases where there are good lines running up the palm, it will usually be found that the subject gives way to occasional fits of intemperance or the desire for drugs. The qualities of the fiery Mount of Mars, from which such a Line of Head starts inside the Life Line, is largely the cause of the peculiarities above indicated. The opposite Mount of Mars (page 141) on the side of the hand, on the contrary, gives mental control, so that even when the Line of Head runs out straight on the palm it partakes of this "Mental Mars" quality, and so denotes that later on in years the subject with such a Line of Head will be able to develop mental control. The sloping Line of Head, however, would denote that the subject allows himself to turn, as it were, away from mental control, and so lets the earlier tendencies become his master.

This point alone is worthy of the consideration of all parents, and if observed by them would do much to help such children to develop mental control over themselves. The accompanying plates show this formation of the Line of Head in all its variations.

THE LINE OF HEAD JOINED TO THE LINE OF LIFE

The position of this line indicates in all cases a highly sensitive disposition, which inclines towards the side of caution and also lacks self-confidence (2–2, Plate I.). Even the cleverest people with this sign seem to rein themselves in too tightly, and are always inclined to undervalue their capabilities and talents.

When, with the same indication, the line is also sloping slightly downwards, the sensitiveness is still more increased. This form is largely found on the hands of artists, painters, and those who even in other walks of life have the sensitive artistic temperament, even though it may not have been developed to a larger extent. If, on the contrary, the Line of Head joined to the Line of Life runs straight out across the hand towards the mental Mount of Mars (2–2, Plate I.), the subject, though still extremely sensitive, has got greater courage of his opinions. Such people do not get credit for being as highly sensitive as do the other people with the line sloping downwards towards the Mount of Imagination. The straighter the Head Line is found, the subject can be more relied on to carry out his determination, and often these highly sensitive and even nervous people are found doing very determined work in connection with some battle for principle or for right which they believe it their moral duty to carry out. If this class of Line of Head, however, go very far across the hand and straight on to the Mental Mount of Mars, it indicates an extremely strong-willed determined person who has the power to hide his sensitiveness and nervousness and stake everything for what he believes his duty to carry out.

The difference in the observation of these two distinct classes of individuals, namely, those with the Line of Head joined but sloping, and the Line of Head joined and straight across the hand, has caused many exponents of this study to make great mistakes in the judgment of their subject. When, as is very often the case, the Line of Head is forked (3–3, Plate II.), also when joined and when these forked lines are equal to one another, especially in cases where the Line of Head is joined to the Line of Life showing the sensitive temperament, this forked mark often indicates a certain want of decision. The subject is inclined to balance too much between the two qualities of brain, the practical and the imaginative. As to what they should do for the best, in such cases it is always wise to advise the subject to act according to first impulse either in dealing with practical or imaginative things. By so doing they employ, as it were, the intuition of the brain, and by using it do not waver and vacillate by too much reasoning over the question or endeavouring to see both sides of it at once. When the sloping Line of Head has a gentle curve downwards towards the Mount of the

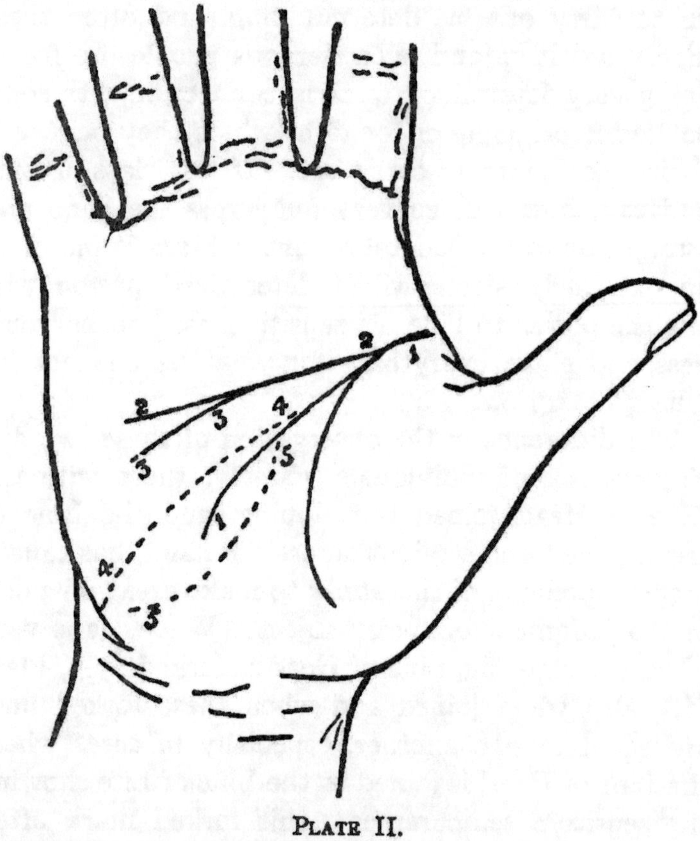

PLATE II.

THE LINE OF HEAD JOINED TO THE LINE OF LIFE AND ITS TERMINATIONS.

Moon (1–1, Plate II.), distinct control over the imagination is indicated. The student will then know that the subject simply uses his imagination when he wishes to do so instead of being controlled by it. But the contrary is the case when the line bends too far down this Mount (4–4, Plate II.). In this case the subject is the slave of his imagination and generally does erratic and peculiar things, or can only work in moods of the moment. People of this latter class seldom, if ever, produce the great results in the world of art or imagination as do those who have the line simply curving downwards into this Mount.

When the Line of the Head bends completely down and turns with a curve, as it were, under the base of the Mount of Luna (5–5, Plate II.), the tendency is to extreme morbid imaginings and such extreme sensitiveness, that people on whose hands it is found generally separate themselves from the rest of their fellows, and either retire from the world altogether and live a solitary life or else make their exit by the gate of suicide. The latter is, in fact, generally the ending of such lives. Their extreme sensitiveness evidently renders life for them almost unbearable. But this formation must not be confounded with the Line of Head curving downwards through the upper part of the Mount (4–4, Plate II.). In this latter case, it can even descend as far down as the wrist itself, and, unless it has an island or star at the end of the line, there is not the danger of suicide. In all such cases, however, there is extreme imagination, extreme sensibility, and a tendency to melancholy and morbidness, but there is no indication of the brain breaking down under strain as there is in the other case of what is known as the distinct tendency for self-murder.

THE LINE OF HEAD SEPARATED FROM THE LINE OF LIFE

The Line of Head is more frequently found connected with than separated from the Line of Life.

When the space is not very wide (3–3, Plate I.), it is an excellent mark to have, giving independence of thought, quickness of judgment, and a certain mental

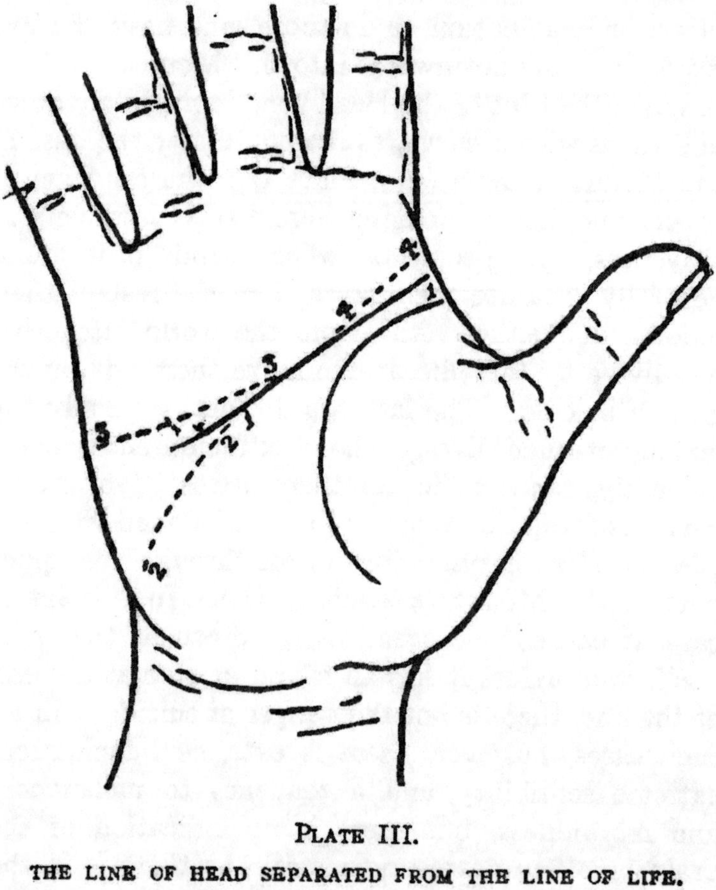

PLATE III.

THE LINE OF HEAD SEPARATED FROM THE LINE OF LIFE.

daring that is invaluable in fighting the battle of life. When the Line of Head is at the same time lying fairly straight across the palm, such individuals have an immense power over others, but their capabilities are always more distinctly shown if they should in any form go in for some kind of public life. People possessing this mark are rather less "hard students" than those with the Line of Head and Line of Life joined together, but they have such brilliancy and quickness of thought that they seem to see in a flash that which takes the other class hard work to attain. But these people with the "open Line of Head" must, above all things, have purpose in their life. Without purpose they are rather like a ship drifting on an idle sea. They may spend their life in an aimless way unless "the call" comes to them or the tide of ambition turns their way and carries them onward.

The same class of line but sloping is the more uncertain of the two characters, because the person is still more inclined to work only by moods. If the mood or the desire does not come, such people, although always brilliant and clever, may often waste their lives doing nothing.

Those people with the Line of Head "open" and ascending slightly upwards towards or on to the Mental Mount of Mars (3–3, Plate III.), are self-appointed leaders, organizers of any public movement. They will sacrifice everything, home, affection, and all ties for what they believe is their public duty in connection with the work that they have undertaken.

The Line of Head very open and separate from the Line of Life denotes a character with too little caution or sensitiveness (4–4, Plate III.). The subject will go to the opposite extreme of him with the Line of Head and Line of Life joined. When the space is very wide it denotes excessive impetuosity and lack of continuity of purpose, a person who pushes himself forward on all occasions, a great desire for notoriety and one continually changing his plans as far as the world is concerned. When this line is excessively open or separate from the Line of Life, the brain seems to be an extremely excitable one. The subject suffers greatly from excessive blood to the head, mental hysteria, sleeplessness, and all things that affect the brain. If the Line of Head is badly formed with islands, or a broad line with breaks and hair lines (1–1, Plate IV.), it is just as much a mark of another form of insanity as the Line of Head curving downwards at the wrist, but with the line mentioned the type is inclined to be morbid with a tendency to suicide.

This other Line of Head with islands indicates the character that will be more likely to be excitable and fly into a temper and kill other people. A Line of Head not too widely separated and either one end of it commencing on the Mount of Jupiter, or with its main branch from the Mount of Jupiter (4–4, Plate III.), is one of the most brilliant marks of all. The student must, however, carefully establish this difference of the Line of Head in his own mind, as well as the termination or the ending of this line. Once he has these two points firmly established, he has gained the great keynote to this subject. When once this part is mastered, he has a sure foundation to work on.

My next remarks will relate to the minor marks and their meaning, and to islands or breaks on or in the Line of Head.

THE LINE OF HEAD AND ITS SECONDARY SIGNS

What are known as "islands" in the Line of Head are very important, especially if they are considered both in relation to the age at which they occur, and also in relation to the mentality itself.

In the first place the principal rule the student must bear in mind is, that islands must be considered as showing a weakness in any line wherever they may be found, and are to be considered unfortunate signs.

On the Line of Head when found in the form of a continuous chain (1–1, Plate IV.), all through the line, they denote mental weakness, but generally produced by ill-health which more immediately affects the brain.

Such mental weakness or "brain illness," if found with nails showing very small "moons" or none at all, denotes an anæmic condition of the blood that affects the brain, a low condition of vitality and bad circulation, which seems to starve the brain of blood and prevents such people from making any continuous effort in regard to study or will power, and causes them to act in an erratic fashion.

If at the same time the Line of Head is seen placed very high on the hand, this sign is worse still in its meaning, and such subjects are inclined to be "half mad" in periods.

When the Line of Head is widely separated from the Line of Life, then this chain formation of islands is still more accentuated and more difficult to cure. Such subjects have periods of mental excitability which it seems impossible for them to control, and in such moments they are liable to fly off at a tangent and commit mad or rash acts, but acts generally dangerous to other people.

When, however, the Line of Head is very sloping (2–2, Plate IV.), with this formation of islands the subject is inclined to have fits of depression and melancholy, during which he is likely to shrink away from people or make an attempt against his own life.

"Suicide while temporarily insane" is the verdict of the jury in such cases.

Another important point of consideration in relation

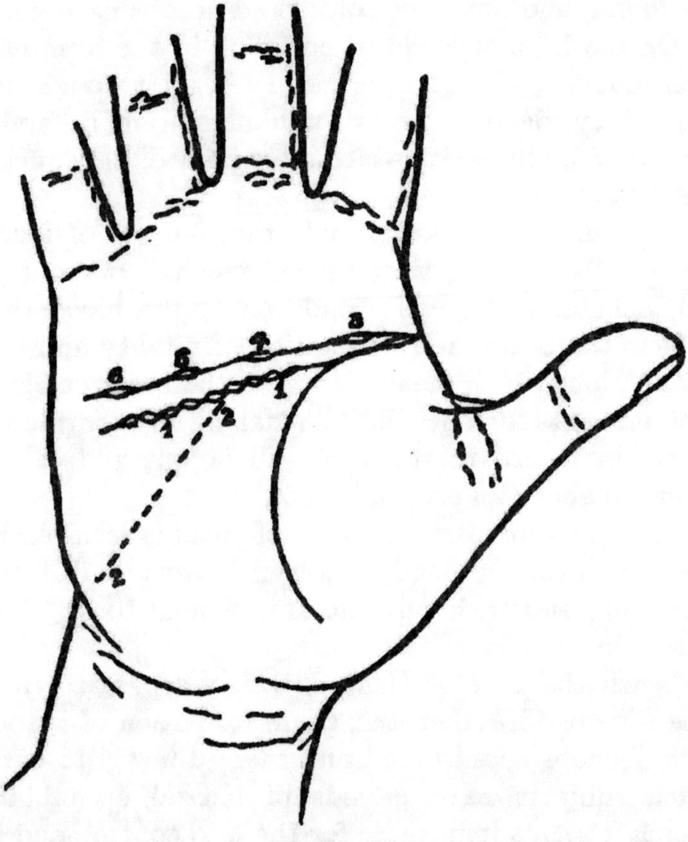

PLATE IV.

ISLANDS ON THE LINE OF HEAD.

to the islands in the Line of Head, is to note their position on the line itself, or under what finger they make their appearance. When these islands are found at the commencement of the line under the first finger or Mount of Jupiter (3, Plate IV.), it will be found that the subject in early life was delicate mentally, and displayed no energy of will; no desire to study, was listless and without ambition.

Under the second finger on the Mount of Saturn (4, Plate IV.), the subject, on the contrary, is inclined to suffer from severe headaches, morbidness, melancholy, and a tendency for inflammation, especially at the base of the head.

If the line looks weak or frays into little hair lines from this point out, it shows that the subject will never recover thoroughly from this malady.

Under the third finger, the Mount of Sun (5, Plate IV.), an island shows a very curious fact, namely that the person is inclined to suffer from weakness of the eyes and short-sight. If many of these islands are marked it generally foreshadows a still greater tendency to blindness and weakness of the sight.

Islands under the fourth finger, the Mount of Mercury (6, Plate IV.), and the extremity of the Head Line denote weakness of the brain in old age, and a highly nervous worrying disposition. If very badly marked they denote that in the latter part of life the subject may be disposed to insanity proceeding from a worrying disposition, and often from the overstraining of the mental faculties. It will thus be seen that every portion of this remarkable line may be divided into sections to obtain marvellous detail in making predictions for the future.

This line can further be divided, showing with considerable clearness the ages at which troubles or changes in the mentality may be expected.

Under the first finger the period of the life indicated is the first 21 years, the second period contains another section of the three 7's, and lasts until 42 years of age; the third period of 7's which will be found under the third finger indicates the section from 49 to 63, and the fourth section which takes in the remainder of the hand, under the fourth finger, stands for the period from 70 up to the end.

CHANGES IN THE LINE OF HEAD

Another extremely interesting point in studying the Line of Head is to take notice of certain changes in its position, or lines either dropping or rising from it, which will also be found to give very remarkable information. For example: if a sloping Line of Head at any point in its track seems to curve or slightly bend upwards (1–1, Plate V.), it indicates that about that period of the person's life some unusual strain will be forced upon him. If this curved line is clearly marked and not interfered with by things that look like blotches in it, the person, although of a completely opposite turn of mind to the practical, will yet rise superior to the occasion, and for the time being will develop a practical or business-like way of looking at things which may even be the very reverse of the nature.

If, however, instead of the curve or bend a fine line is seen leaving the Head Line in an upward direction (2–2, Plate V.), that period will leave a definite mark on the subject's entire character for the remainder of his life. In some cases these fine lines will, after a few years, appear to develop more strongly, and may even become a kind of second Head Line. This would denote that the person continues to cultivate the practical side of his nature that was at that period called into existence.

If one were examining a straight Line of Head and

noticed a curve downward or a fine line growing downwards from it (3–3, Plate V.), the natural interpretation of such a mark would be that at that date

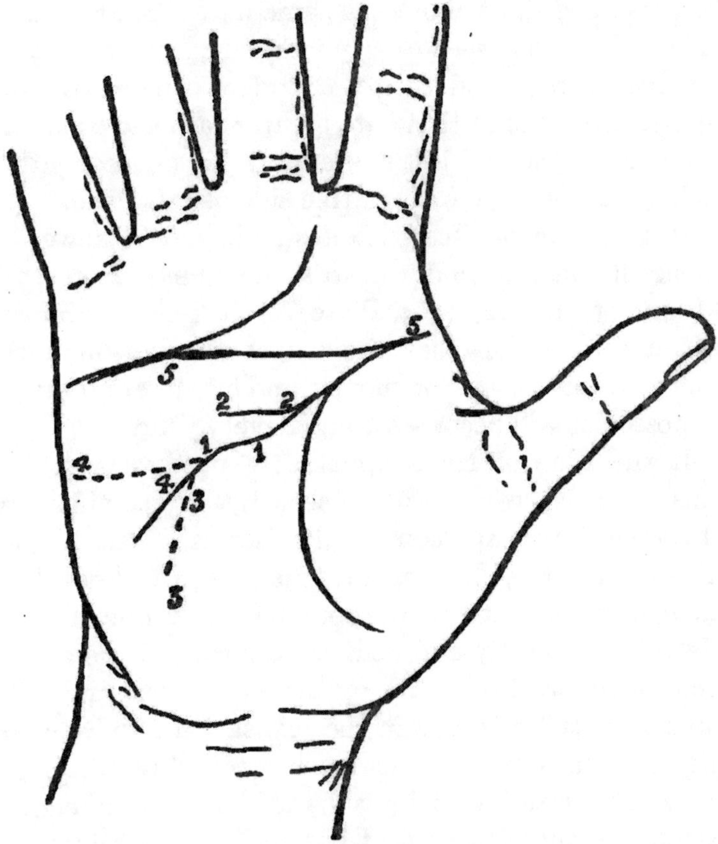

PLATE V.

MORE VARIATIONS OF THE LINE OF HEAD.

in the person's career he had become less practical, or for the time being developed the more imaginative qualities of the mentality. In this latter case, curiously enough, it often denotes that the person had at that period of his life become more wealthy or prosperous, and so he was able to develop the artistic side of his nature. It is logical to assume that he could only have done this if the strain in the practical battle had been lessened about that time, but this must only be presumed if, at about the same date, the Sun Line (Plate XV.) were seen clearly marked or suddenly appearing on the hand, then the student can be positive in assuming that at that date greater ease and comfort came into the subject's life and he consequently turned to the more imaginative side of existence.

If the Line of Head itself should curve upward, especially at the end towards the fourth finger or Mount of Mercury (4–4, Plate V.), it denotes almost without exception that the longer the person lives the more his desire for money and his determination to possess it will become stronger every year.

If the Line of Head apparently partly leaves its natural place, which will be seen by an examination of the left hand, and completely rises as it were to the Line of Heart (5–5, Plate V.), the person will develop an enormous fixity of purpose for some one desire. He will apparently and deliberately control the affectionate side of his nature by his will power, and will stick at nothing to obtain the realisation of whatever his desire may be. If this mark is found on a square thick-set material looking hand, it is a foregone conclusion that the subject has set his determination on some material object, such as wealth, and he will stop at nothing, even crime, in carrying out his aim. If this mark is found on a long hand the object of the ambition is certain to be connected with intellectual power over people and absolute determination to accomplish whatever the purpose of the career may be.

This mark must not be confounded with one clear

line running across the hand from side to side (Plate VI.), because in this case the Line of Head has not

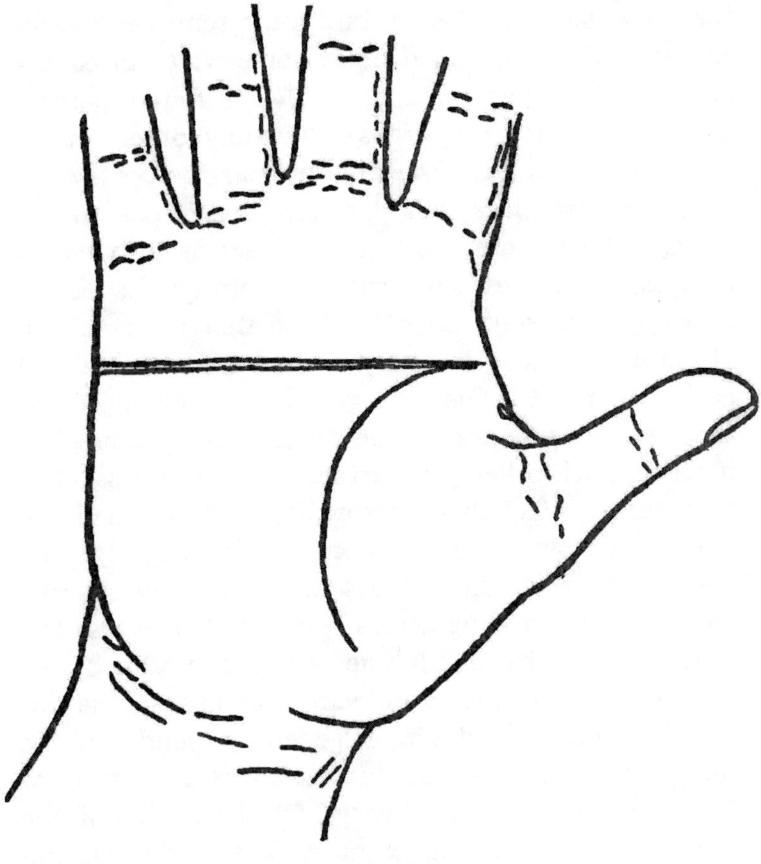

PLATE VI.

THE LINE OF HEAD AND THE LINE OF HEART RUNNING TOGETHER.

risen out of its position, but simply denotes tremendous intensity of character, for good or evil as the case may be; such a person would exhibit great power of concentration, and if he concentrated his mentality on any purpose he would unite with it his heart nature. But if he had set his heart or affections on any person, he would unite with that desire the whole force of his mental nature. In this case it is as if these two sides of the mentality, the sentimental and the mental, were linked or in some way united together. Such persons I have always found possess greater intensity of purpose than any other, but I have never found it a very happy mark to possess.

In the first place, this peculiar type of person appears to be so rare in life that he seems to have no companions and for that reason has always the feeling of being intensely lonely and isolated from others. He is usually also in every way super-sensitive and easily wounded in his feelings. I have seldom found these people successful, unless when acting alone, but if linked with others by partnership in business, etc., they seem to feel their personality cramped, and the partnership as a rule seldom results happily. In considering this, the student must carefully observe whether this one line across the hand lies across the centre where the Head Line would naturally be, or whether it lies higher up towards the base of the fingers where the Heart Line is generally found. If the former case, one may be sure that it is a question of head and mentality and very little heart; but if the latter, it is a question of more intensity of feeling emotion and affection than of mental intensity.

CROSSES AND SQUARES IN CONNECTION WITH THE LINE OF HEAD

Small, sharply-defined crosses in any position just over or touching the Line of Head are generally signs of accidents to the Head itself.

Under Jupiter (1, Plate VII.), they usually are brought about by blows caused generally by the subject's desire to rule and to be too dogmatic or tyrannical.

Under Saturn (2, Plate VII.), crosses indicate injuries to the head from accidents by animals, blows by treachery, mine explosions, etc., and generally relate to accidents of a treacherous nature.

Under the Mount of the Sun (3, Plate VII.), these crosses have been found to relate to accidents to the head from sudden falls, such as the subject striking his head by falling, concussion of the brain, etc.

Under the Mount of Mercury (4, Plate VII.), these sharply defined crosses relate to injuries to the head due to accidents generally produced by scientific experiments or some hazardous business venture.

Small defined squares touching the Line of Head (5, Plate VII.), are in all cases signs of preservation, and they relate to the particular qualities of the Mount of the hand under which they are found. (*See* chapter on Mounts, page 140.)

DOUBLE LINES OF HEAD

Double Lines of Head (6–6, Plate VII.), are as rarely found as are cases of the single line right across the hand. In all cases where the Double Line of Head stands out distinct and clear as two separate lines, the object will be found to have a dual mentality. He is usually capable of an enormous amount of mental work and is of that class of people who carry out two separate mental lives with success. It is often found with one line joined to the Line of Life and the other rising from the Mount of Jupiter; if such is the case, the interpretation would be that one side of the nature is extremely sensitive and cautious, while the other is self-confident with a great desire to rule or enforce its mental ideas on the world.

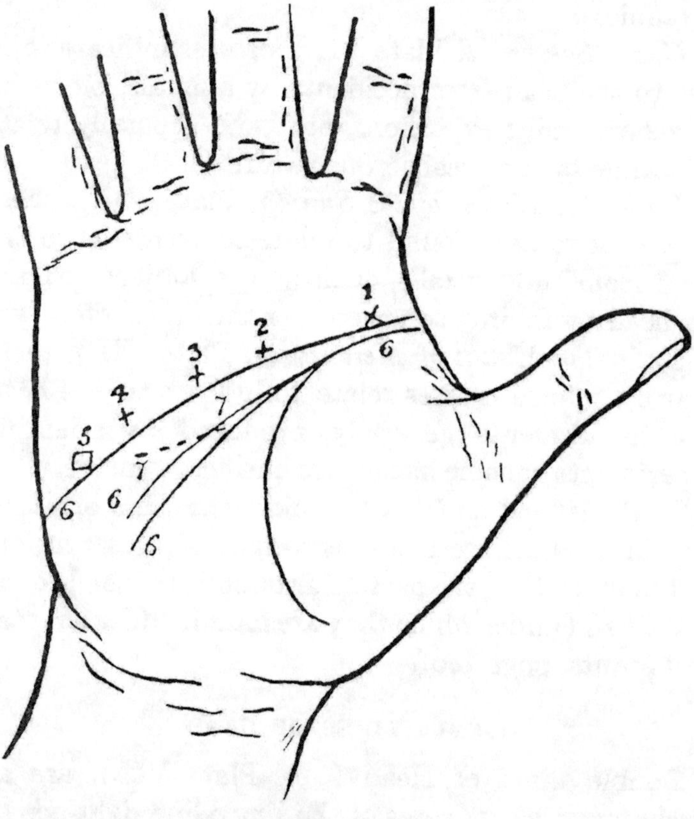

PLATE VII.

DOUBLE LINES OF HEAD, ALSO CROSSES AND SQUARES.

Although such a sign as the Double Line of Head gives a remarkable degree of mentality, yet I have always found it a more successful sign to find one clear Line of Head well marked on the hand than the two Lines of Head in any of their positions.

Another form of the Double Line of Head (7–7,

Plate VII.), is one where the main line seems to separate about the middle of the hand, and where one branch goes across the hand and the other descends towards the Mount of the Moon. In such a case we get the double mental personality, but one which is more under the control of the will of the subject, whereas the two double distinct lines denote that the two mental personalities seem to act independently one from the other.

It has been considered by many ancient authorities that the Double Line of Head, when found with two distinct lines, is a sign of the inheritance of great riches or power. I have generally found, however, that what it means is, that although the financial results of such a person's life may be either great wealth or power, yet he may inherit it from his mental right and not from his birth right.

THE LINE OF HEAD ON THE SEVEN TYPES OF HANDS

There are seven distinct types of hands, bearing in their own way more or less relationship to the Seven Races of Humanity (page 118).

These seven types of hands are as follows:

I.—The Elementary or Lowest type.
II.—The Square, also called the Useful or Practical.
III.—The Spatulate or Active.
IV.—The Philosophic.
V.—The Conic or Artistic.
VI.—The Psychic or Idealistic.
VII.—The Mixed Hand.

As a rule the Line of Head is generally found in accordance with the type of hand on which it is seen, namely, lying straight or what is called "level-headed" on the Square-looking or Practical hand; or sloping, and thus indicating the more imaginative qualities on the Philosophic, Conic, or Psychic types.

Consequently, if it be found on a hand in what may be called opposition to its class, such a Line of Head immediately possesses a greater significance.

For example, if a sloping Line of Mentality were seen on the Square or Practical hand, it would indicate that though the bases of that man or woman's thoughts and plans were of the practical kind, yet they possessed a far greater power of imagination than any casual observer would at first sight give them credit for.

On the contrary, if the Line of Head were found straight or level on the Spatulate, Philosophic, Conic, or Psychic types, it would denote that the person in question was usually level-headed and practical, even in their highest dreams of philosophy or idealistic creations.

On the Elementary hand the Line of Head is usually found short, straight, and coarse-looking, often nothing more than a short deep-set furrow. Consequently, if found long and clear, it would indicate a superior mental development in a coarse, brutal or animal nature.

If in a Square-looking hand the Line of Head were found sloping instead of long and straight, it would denote an unusual development of the artistic and imaginative qualities, but always with the practical and logical basis for its support.

On the Spatulate hand the natural indication of the

Line of Head is long, clear and sloping, but if found straight or level it would indicate a practical development of the brain endeavouring to set off the active energy and originality indicated by the Spatulate formation.

On the Philosophic type, the hand of the thinker and philosopher, the usual position of the Line of Mentality is long and sloping, but if found straight or level it indicates a mental development of the logical and practical qualities which might not be expected in such a class or type.

The same rules hold good with the Conic and Psychic, but with what is called the Mixed type, the best Line of Head to find would be one, long straight and level-looking, because this class, being a mixture as it were of all the others, would require a practical or level-headed mentality to hold its own amid the mixture of tendencies which the last type personifies.

CHAPTER III

THE LINE OF LIFE AND ITS VARIATIONS

THE Line of Life is that line which runs round the base of the thumb and lies directly over a large blood-vessel called the great Palmer Arch (1–1, Plate VIII.). This blood-vessel is more directly connected with the heart, stomach, and vital organs which may have given use to its term "The Vital," as used by the ancients.

It is reasonable to assume that it is this intimate connection with the vital organs of the body which enables it to foretell the length of life from *natural causes*.

If the student will bear this in mind it will make clear and plain to him many difficulties in connection with predictions as to health and disease, and he will follow more easily the following explanations.

The first rules to master are, that to be normal the Line of Life should be long, clearly marked, and without any irregularities or breaks of any kind. Such a formation would indicate length of life, vitality, freedom from illness, and strength of constitution (1–1, Plate VIII.).

Bearing the first observation in mind it will be noticed that as the Line of Life represents the stomach and the vital organs, when well marked the stomach and digestion must necessarily be in a good condition.

When made up of little pieces or linked like a chain,

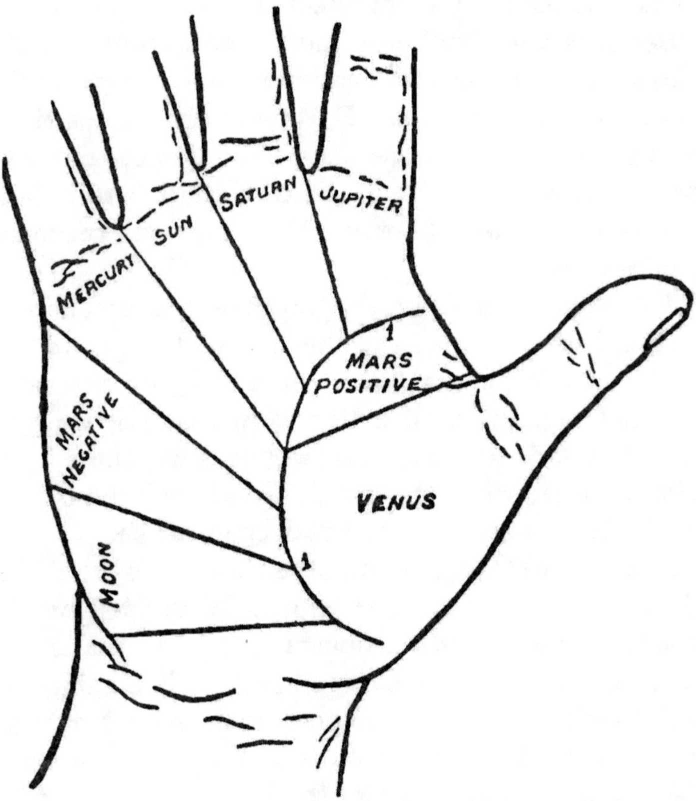

PLATE VIII.

THE LINE OF LIFE AND SECTIONS OF INFLUENCES FROM THE MOUNTS.

it is a certain sign of poor health, weak stomach and lack of vitality.

At this point I must ask the most careful attention to the following rules—which no other book on the subject contains, and which I have not published in any of my other writings, viz.: as the Line of Life seems in every sense to be the representative on the hand of the body or trunk of the man—so the position of these breaks, marks, links, or islands denotes the portion of the body most affected.

Before we go further I must also impress on the student to grasp the fact that every line or sign on the hand plays a dual rôle. By one of their rôles these lines indicate the disease the person is most liable to for the entire run of the life, and in another rôle these lines indicate the date when the illness will reach its greatest gravity.

To explain carefully this strange phenomenon of nature, I have divided this line into sections (*see* Plate VIII.), and although I am not writing on astrology in these pages, yet all believers in that science may be interested to find how wonderfully these twin sciences agree when the comparison is pointed out by an impartial observer such as I claim to be.

In Plate VIII. are shown the Sections of the Line of Life with their various tendencies divided by the mounts at the base of the fingers. This will materially assist the student to comprehend their significance and, together with the influence of the month of birth as set out in the chapters on the Mounts of the Hand (page 140), will enable him to obtain an accuracy on all matters relating to health, diseases, and dangers to the life that up till now has never been attained.

We will now proceed to consider the details as regards the Line of Life itself.

THE LINE OF LIFE

It is very important at the outset to consider the qualities of this very important line. In some hands it is broad and shallow on the surface of the hand, in others it is deep and fine; the appearance of this line is very often deceptive, and leads students astray when they have not had their attention called to its appearance.

The broad, shallow Line of Life often leads people to suppose that it is a sign of a very healthy, robust constitution; but, on the contrary, such an indication is not nearly as good a sign as a clear, thin, deep line. The broad Life Line seems to belong to people who have more robust animal strength, whereas the finer line relates to people who have more nerve or will-force. Under any strain of ill-health, it is the finer line that will hold out, whereas the broad-looking line has not the same resisting force.

Very broad lines on the hand denote more muscular strength than will power, and I cannot impress this difference too strongly on the minds of my readers. If the line is made of chain formation (1–1, Plate IX.), it is a sure sign of a tendency to bad health, and especially so if the hand be soft. The same marks on a hard, firm hand would not indicate as much delicacy, because hard, firm hands denote in themselves a robust constitution.

Another important point to consider is, whether the Line of Life goes straight up to the side of the Mount of Venus and narrows that Mount (2–2, Plate IX.), or whether it forms a well-defined curve or semicircle out into the palm (3–3, Plate IX.). In the first case it indicates a naturally more delicate constitution, and less force of animal magnetism. This explanation will be readily understood by readers when I again call their attention to the fact that one of the most important blood-vessels going from the body to the hand is called the Great Palmer Arch, which carries the blood up to the hand towards the root of the

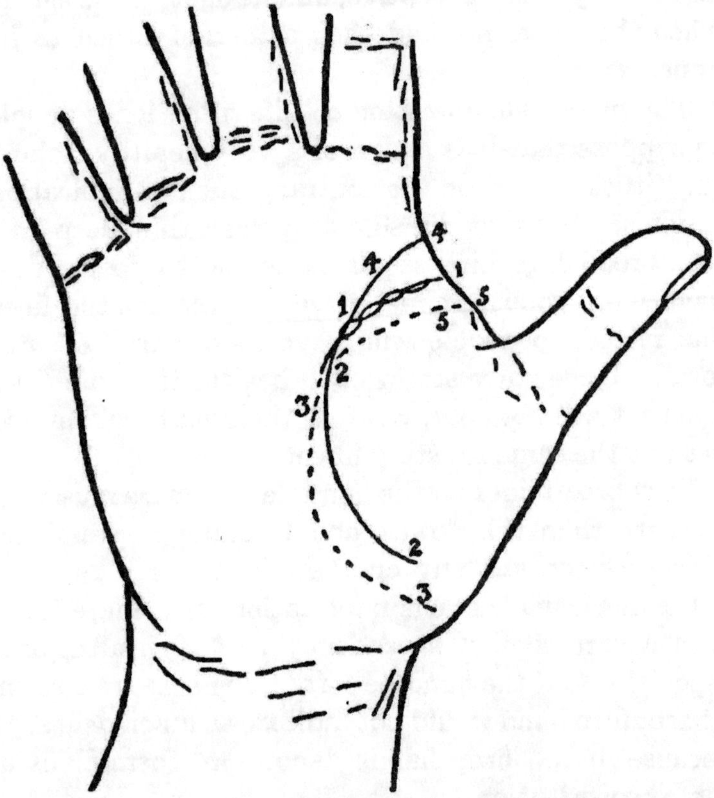

PLATE IX.

THE LINE OF LIFE AND ITS VARIATIONS.

thumb, and carries the circulation back on the other side of the Arch almost underneath the Line of Life. It will, therefore, be seen that people who have a weaker constitution are more likely to have this Great Palmer Arch narrower in construction than those who have a robust constitution and strong circulation of the blood. This is the reason why, when the Mount of Venus is large and wide on the hand, it gives rise to the idea that it indicates a more passionate animal nature than when this mount is thin and narrow.

While speaking on this particular point, I must also call attention to the fact that when the Line of Head is curved downwards instead of running straight across the palm, that it seems to be more attracted to the qualities indicated by the Mount of Venus and gives more to the imaginative, romantic nature, showing a greater tendency to fall in love, than with people who possess the Line of Head running straight across the hand, as if it were not attracted to the qualities indicated by the Mount of Venus. It will thus be seen that every point of this study bearing on character can be reasoned out from a logical standpoint. This places the study upon a higher foundation than when it is considered purely from the superstitious standpoint with which it has so long been associated.

If the Line of Life is seen to rise high on the hand towards the Mount of Jupiter (4–4, Plate IX.), the subject has more control over himself, and his life is more governed by the ambitious side of his nature. When, however, the Line of Life rises lower down on the palm, more from the Mount of Mars (5–5, Plate IX.), it gives less control over the temper. When this sign is noticed, especially in the case of young persons, it will be found that they are more quarrelsome, more disobedient, and have less ambition in connection with their studies.

ASCENDING LINES

When the Line of Life is found with a number of ascending lines, even if they are small, it denotes a life of greater energy; and the dates at which these lines ascend from the Line of Life may always be considered points at which the subject has made a particular effort towards whatever may have been the special purpose of his destiny at that moment. When these lines are seen ascending towards or on the Mount of Jupiter (1–1, Plate X.), it indicates the desire and ambition to rise in life, especially in some way that would give the subject control or authority over others. If one of the lines be found partly arrested or stopped at the Line of Head (2–2, Plate X.), it indicates that the subject has by some mental error of judgment or stupidity, broken or prevented the effort, which started well, from reaching a successful termination. If one of these lines reaches and stops at the Line of Heart, it indicates that the affections have, or will, interfere with the subject's special effort in whatever direction this line indicates. If one of these lines crosses and joins the line of Fate (3–3, Plate X.), it indicates and gives two distinct dates which are very curious in their meaning. The first date it gives is when this line leaves the Line of Life on its way towards the Line of Fate. The date of this start towards the Line of Fate will be given on the Line of Fate itself, right opposite where this line begins to grow from the Line of Life. This mark will denote that the subject has made a determined effort at that moment in his career to make his own destiny, and to break free from the circumstances or people that surround him or tie him down.

It is always a successful sign when this line is found to join the Line of Fate, especially if the Line of Fate looks stronger at or about this point of the junction.

The second date is given at the period in the Line

of Life when one is reading down the Line of Life itself. The singular point about this is that a repetition of circumstances will be found to occur in the destiny. Suppose, for example, one saw this line going towards the Fate Line at twenty-six years of age —a circumstance or repetition of the occurrence will be found to occur at almost double that age, namely, fifty-two years of age, which would give a more or less exact date of this occurrence when reading the Line of Life. As an illustration to help the reader I may say that I have generally found that this mark will indicate that the subject has, in the first instance, broken free from some tie at an early date, and that a similar occurrence will take place at the second date, viz., late in life, when again the subject seems to break free from some tie, and goes out more into the world for himself.

This curious sign very often helps in deciding matters as regards marriage. The man, or woman, will apparently assert his independence more, and leave the ties of home life, and again go out in the world and fight the battle for himself, as he did in the earlier part of his existence, when he probably left his parents' influence and forged ahead for himself.

When the ascending line is seen crossing over towards the Mount of Saturn, and running as an independent line not joined to the Line of Fate (6, Plate X.), it will be found that the subject has carried out a kind of second fate. The date when this line left the Line of Life will give the first date of its commencement, *i.e.*, opposite it on the Fate Line. If the line be a good one it would give its second date when reading down the Line of Life, where, if the line were good, it carried out this second fate to a successful culmination.

CHAPTER IV

THE LINE OF MARS OR INNER LIFE LINE

WHAT is called the Line of Mars is that line that is found only on some hands encircling the Mount of Venus and inside the Line of Life.

This Line, which rises on the Mount of Mars, from which it derives its name, when found clear and strong appears to back up and reinforce the Line of Life (4–4, Plate X.). It indicates great vitality, power of resistance to illness and disease, and is not found on all hands.

It is an excellent sign on the hands of soldiers, or in connection with all persons who follow a dangerous calling.

All breaks or bad marks indicated on the Line of Life are minimized on the hands that have this Inner Life Line, or Line of Mars.

As its name implies, in character it denotes a robust and rather fighting disposition, a person naturally inclined to rush into dangers and quarrels, and if deeply marked and reddish in colour it increases all indications of accidents and dangers shown on other parts of the hand.

When a branch seems to shoot off from this line and runs on to the Mount of Luna (5–5, Plate X.), it foreshadows restlessness and an intense craving for excitement. With a weak-looking Line of Mentality it is a sure sign of a craving for drink and intemperance of all kinds, and at the point where it breaks through

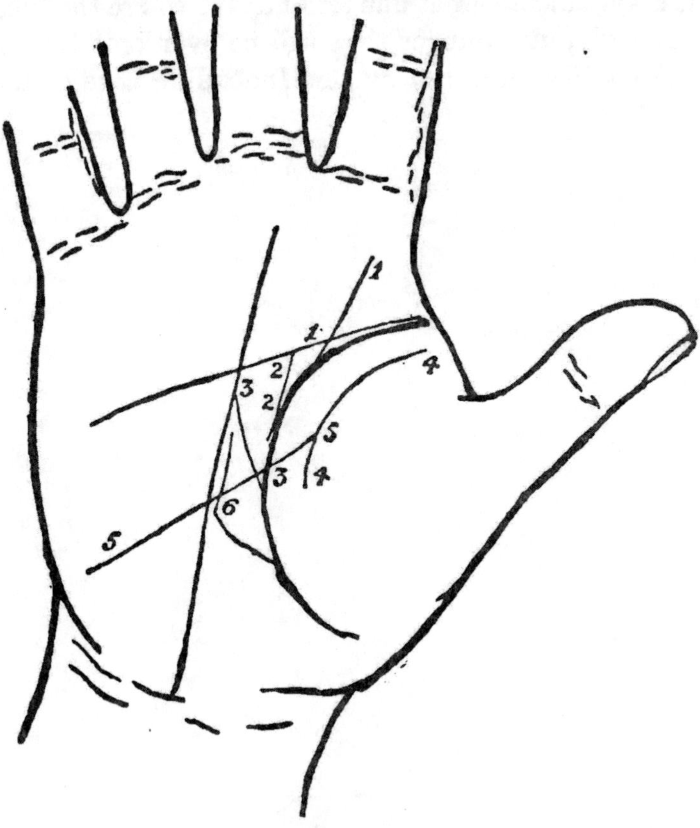

PLATE X.

THE LINE OF LIFE, THE LINE OF MARS, AND OTHER SIGNS.

the Line of Life, it generally indicates death brought on by the intemperance this mark foreshadows.

It is generally found on short, thick-set square hands or short hands, but when found on a long, thin, and narrow palm, it indicates great vitality and resistance to disease, a nervous, highly-strung, and rather irritable disposition.

Any broken Life Line with this Line of Mars behind it may indicate great danger of death where the break appears, but a danger that will be overcome through the vitality indicated by this Inner Life Line or Line of Mars.

CHAPTER V

THE LINE OF DESTINY OR FATE

THE Line of Destiny, otherwise called the Line of Fate (1–1, Plate XI.) is naturally one of the most important of the principal lines of the hand.

Although one may never be able to explain why it is, this line undoubtedly appears to indicate at least the main events of one's career.

It may be found on the hand even at the moment of birth, clearly indicating the class of Fate or Destiny that lies in the far distant future before the individual.

In some cases it may look faint or shadowy, as if the path of Destiny were not yet clearly defined, while in other instances almost every step of the road is chiselled out with its milestones of failure or success, sorrow or joy, as the case may be.

That some human beings seem to be more children of Fate than others has been admitted by almost all thinkers, but why they should be so has been the great question that baffles all students of such subjects.

There are some who appear to have no Fate, and others who seem to carve their Destiny from day to day.

I have seen hundreds of cases where every step of the journey was indicated from childhood to the grave; others where only the principal changes in the career were marked in advance. There are, again, others where nothing seemed decided, and where the events indicated by the Line of Fate appeared to change from year to year.

The why and wherefore of such things may be impossible to fathom, but there are so many mysteries in Life itself that one more or less does not seem to matter.

Some of the greatest teachers and philosophers have come to the conclusion that Fate exists for all. In the 17th Article of Religion in the Episcopal Church it is stated, and in no uncertain manner, that "Predestination to life is the everlasting purpose of God." All through the Bible the Destiny of nations and of men is clearly laid down, and from the first chapter of Genesis to the last page of Revelation the trials, tribulations, and pathway of the Jews was prophesied and predicted ages in advance.

Thousands of years before the birth of Christ, it was foretold in Holy Writ in what manner He should be born, and in what manner He should die. It was predicted that a Virgin should conceive and that a Judas should betray, and that both were necessary "that the Scriptures might be fulfilled."

In more recent ages thousands and thousands of predictions have been fulfilled, and all point to some mysterious agency that underlies the purpose of humanity, and that nothing from the smallest to the greatest is left to blind chance.

It may be that the Soul—in being part of the Universal Soul of all things—*knows all things*, and so through the instrumentality of the brain writes its knowledge of the Future in advance.

To the mysteries of the mind there are no limits. Medical science has, in late years, gone so far as to prove that there must be an advance growth or change in the brain cells years before action or change in character become the result of such development. For all we know, every deed in our careers is the result of some such mental change, and as there are more super-sensitive nerves from the brain to the hand, it may then follow that such changes and subsequent actions in our lives may be written in our hands even long years in advance.

It may be, then, that to all living beings there is a Destiny "that shapes our ends, rough hew them as we will."

I would, however, humbly suggest that each of us endeavour by knowledge to find what our Fate may be, and like loyal workmen accept whatever the task should prove, and so carry it out to the utmost of our ability, willing to leave the final result to the Master that thought fit to employ us in the working out of His design.

All such questions as these the student of this subject must settle in his own mind, for when he or she once broaches this study of Fate, he will be assailed on all sides, and the student must be prepared to give "an answer for the faith that is in him."

In studying the hand it will be found that the Line of Fate may rise from the following distinct positions:

It may rise from and out of the Line of Life (2–2, Plate XI.), straight up from the wrist (1–1, Plate XI.), from the Mount of the Moon (3–3, Plate XI.), or from the middle of the palm.

The following is the meaning of these principal positions:

RISING FROM THE LINE OF LIFE

Rising from the Line of Life (2–2, Plate XI.), the subject's success will be made by personal effort and merit; the early years of such a Fate will be cramped and difficult; circumstances and the early surroundings will not be favourable, and such people will be greatly hampered or sacrificed to the wishes and plans of their parents or relatives. If the Line of Fate, however, should run on clear and strong from where it leaves the Line of Life, then the subject will overcome all such difficulties and win success by his own personal effort and merit, and not depend on what is termed luck at any time in the career.

Another striking and important point is that the date or years marked on the Line of Fate of such a breaking out into the palm, will be found to coincide with the year in the subject's life in which he asserted his independence or launched out into what he more particularly wanted to do. (*See* also end of chapter on Time, page 112.)

In any case this date as indicated will be found to be one of the most important in his career.[1]

RISING FROM THE WRIST

When the Line of Fate rises from the Wrist (1–1, Plate XI.) and goes straight up the centre of the palm to the Mount of Saturn, provided at the same time the Line of Sun (4–4, Plate XI.) is found well marked, luck, brilliance, and success will attend the Destiny, and extreme good fortune may be anticipated.

[1] For how to obtain dates and years *see* Chapter XIX.

RISING FROM THE MOUNT OF THE MOON

Rising from the Mount of the Moon (3–3, Plate XI.) the Fate will be more eventful, changeable, and largely depending on the fancy and caprice of other people.

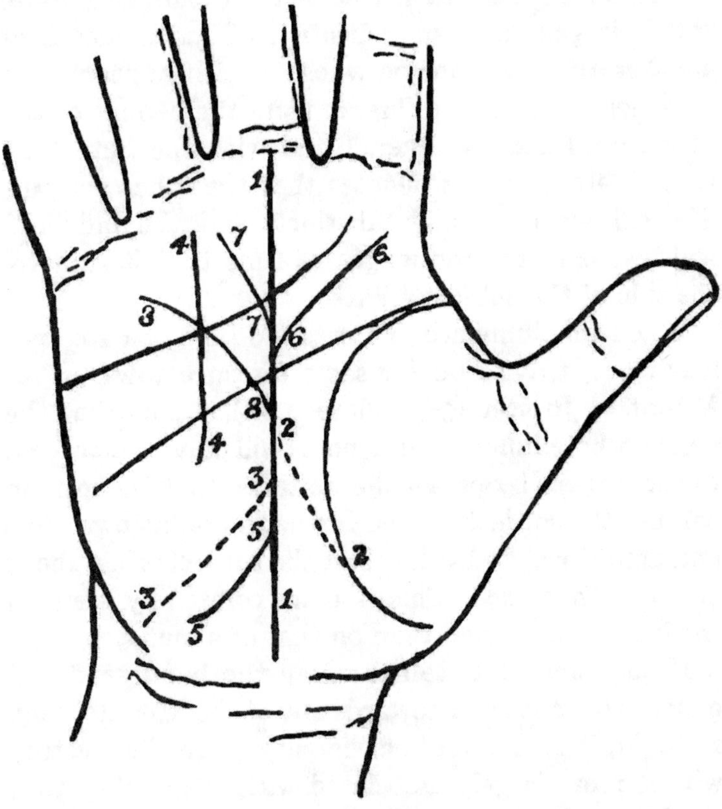

PLATE XI.

THE LINE OF DESTINY AND ITS MODIFICATIONS.

If such a line be found joining the Line of Heart (1–1, Plate XII.), it foretells a happy and prosperous marriage, but one in which idealism, romance, and some fortunate circumstances play their rôle, and one which results more from the caprice or fancy of the person of the other sex.

If the Line of Fate be itself straight but with a line running in and joining it from the Mount of the Moon (5–5, Plate XI.), it indicates that the influence of some outside person has helped the subject's Fate, and it is generally an indication of the influence of another sex to the one on whose hand it appears.

When this line of influence from the Mount of the Moon does not, however, blend with the Fate Line (2–2, Plate XII.), it denotes that the other person's life will always remain distinct, and the influence will last only for the length of time that it runs by the side of the subject's Fate.

When this influence line cuts the Line of Fate and, leaving it, travels on for some distance towards the Mount of Jupiter (3–3, Plate XII.) it tells that the person whose influence it denotes will only be attracted to the subject by personal ambition—that this person will use the subject for the furthering of his own aims and ambitions, and will desert the subject when she is of no further use. This is more commonly seen on the hand of a woman than on that of a man.

If the Line of Fate ascending the hand sends an offshoot from it on or towards any of the Mounts, such as to Jupiter, the Sun, or Mercury, then the Destiny will be more largely associated with the quality that the Mount it approaches symbolises.

For example: If such a line be seen approaching or going towards Jupiter (6–6, Plate XI.) it denotes responsibility, power of command over others, or some high position which will commence to be realised from the date when the offshoot leaves the Line of Fate. If such a mark continues its course and finishes on the Mount of Jupiter, it is one of the most magnificent signs of success that can be found for that particular aim or purpose.

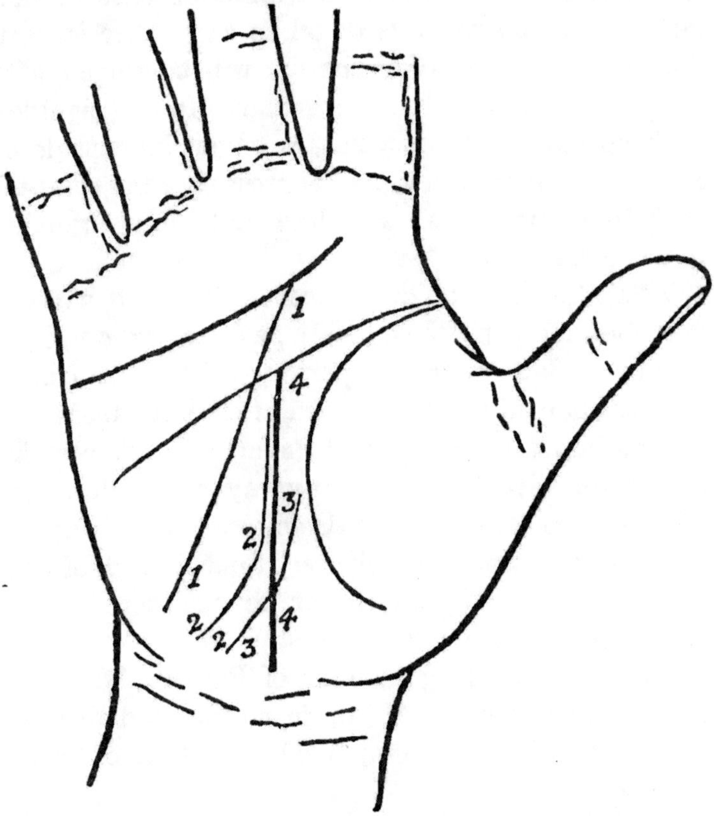

PLATE XII.

THE LINE OF DESTINY AND ITS VARIATIONS.

If this offshoot ascends towards the Mount of the Sun (7–7, Plate XI.) the success will be in the direction of riches and public life, which will give great publicity or renown; this is also a magnificent sign of success.

If the offshoot goes towards the Mount of Mercury (8–8, Plate XI.), the success it indicates will be more in the direction of some special achievement either in science or commerce.

If the Line of Fate itself should not ascend towards its habitual position on the Mount of Saturn, but, instead, run up towards or on to any other Mount, then the whole effort of the life will be tinged with whatever quality that particular Mount signifies. Such an indication must not, however, be considered as the certain or sure sign of success as when the Line of Fate keeps to its own place and sends branches to some particular Mount.

When the Line of Fate ascends the hand without branches and runs like a lonely path up and on to the Mount of Saturn, such a person will be like a child of Fate chained to an iron road of circumstances. It will be impossible for him to avert the trials of his Destiny or mitigate them in any way. He will receive no help from others, and little will ever happen except to bring him sorrow or tragedy. Such a mark of Fate through the hand must never be considered as "a good line of Destiny."

To have a really good Line of Fate it should not be too heavily marked, but just clear and distinct, and, above all, be accompanied by a Line of Sun in some form or other.

If a Line of Fate run over the Mount of Saturn and up into the base of the finger, it is an unfortunate sign, as everything the subject undertakes will get out of his control, and he will not apparently know how or when to stop in whatever he takes up.

When the Line of Fate appears to be stopped by the Line of Heart, the career will always be ruined through or by the affections being badly placed.

When, however, it joins the Line of Heart and they

together ascend the Mount of Jupiter (1–1, Plate XII.), the subject will have happiness through his affections and will be helped by love and affection to attain his highest ambitions. He will also be extremely lucky through the friendship and love of those he meets, and will be greatly benefited and helped by others.

When the Line of Fate appears to be stopped by the Line of Head (4–4, Plate XII.), it foretells that his career will be spoiled by the subject's own stupidity or mental foolishness.

RISING FROM THE MIDDLE OF THE PALM

When the Line of Fate only makes its appearance far up in the centre of the palm, in what is called the Plain of Mars, it indicates a hard early life and that the subject must always have a hard fight to gain his ends; but should the Line ascend clearly and strongly from the Plain of Mars and have a branch to or on towards the Mount of the Sun, such a person will be the architect of his own fortunes, and without help or assistance will win success and fortune by his own personal hard work and merit.

When the Line of Fate rises from the Line of Head and when it is well marked, everything will come to the subject late in life and only then by his own brains.

When the Line of Fate is seen with one branch on the Mount of Venus and the other on the Mount of the Moon (1–2, Plate XIII.) it indicates a career of romance and passion, by which the whole of the Destiny will be swayed.

When the Line of Fate itself rises inside the Life

Line on the Mount of Venus (2–2, Plate XIII.), passionate love will affect the whole career, and such persons, it will be found, usually place their affections on impossible people or on those who are in some way

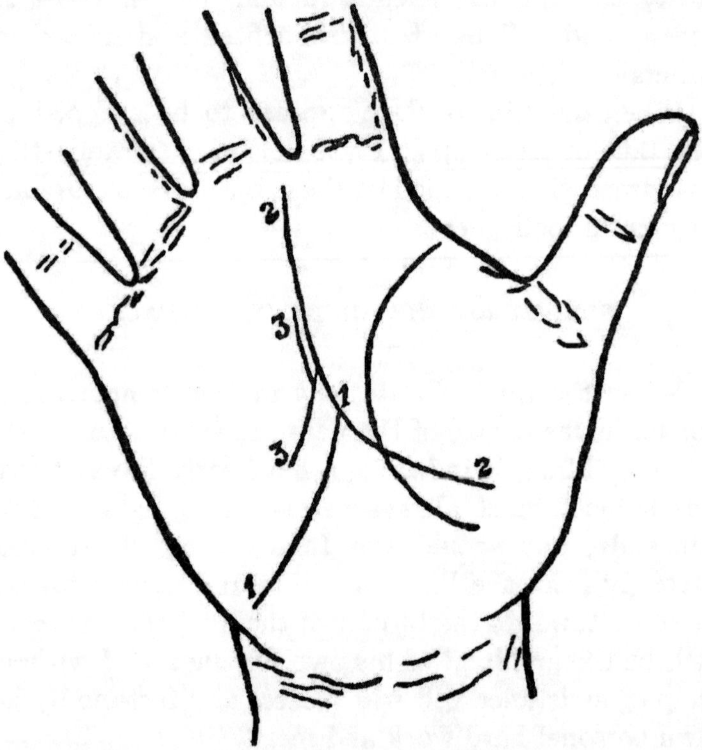

PLATE XIII.

THE LINE OF DESTINY AND ITS MODIFICATIONS.

tied up by marriage or who otherwise are unable to gratify the love that the other person demands. This is a most unlucky sign for affection to find in the hands of a woman.

When the Line of Fate is broken or made up in little bits, the career will be found full of troubles, breaks, and nothing that one gets will last long enough to bring any settled or continuous success.

A break in the Fate Line is not always a bad sign to have, provided that one side begins before the other ends; in such a case it foretells a complete change in surroundings and position, and if the new line looks good and straight it will be found to mean that the change will bring about an advancement in position commencing at the date when the second line first makes its appearance.[1]

INFLUENCE LINES

When any small line joins the Fate Line or goes on with it as an attendant line, such a mark usually indicates marriage at the date when these lines join (3-3, Plate XIII.). If, on the contrary, these lines do not join, marriage with the person is not likely to occur although the affection and influence will be present in the career.

When one of these influence lines appears by the side of the Fate Line and crosses through it towards or on to the Mount of Mars, it indicates that the influence thus shown will turn to hate and will injure the career of the person on whose hand it is found (1-1, Plate XIV.).

DOUBLE LINES OF FATE

When the Line of Fate is itself double (2-2, Plate XIV.), it is a sign of what is called "a double life," but if, after running side by side for some length

[1] For dates on the Line of Fate *see* Chapter XIX.

these two lines join or become one, it foretells that "the double life" has been caused by some great affection, that circumstances prevented a union, but that the preventing cause will be removed at the point where these two lines join.

When, however, a double Line of Fate is clearly marked, especially if they incline towards different mounts of the hand, such a mark indicates that two careers would be carried out simultaneously—one perhaps as a hobby and the other as the principal career.

When the Line of Fate is extremely faint or just barely traced through the palm, it will be found to indicate a general disbelief in the idea of Fate and Destiny. It is often found on the hands of very materialistic persons, those who rebel against the idea that they are governed in any way by Fate or by any power save themselves.

When this is found, and at the same time a good clear Line of Head, such people will be sure to win success by their mentality alone, but the details of their destiny will not be able to be told, and one must content oneself with chiefly describing their characteristics, peculiarities, etc.

When no Line of Fate whatever is found and only a very ordinary Line of Head, then there will be nothing very particular to say about the Destiny; such people, as a rule, lead very colourless lives, nothing seems to affect them much one way or the other, and they will be found to have very little purpose to illumine the drab monotony of their existence.

An island (3, Plate XIV.) is an extremely bad sign to find in the Line of Fate.

When found at the very beginning of the line (4,

Plate XIV.) it indicates some mystery regarding the commencement of such careers, such as illegitimate birth.

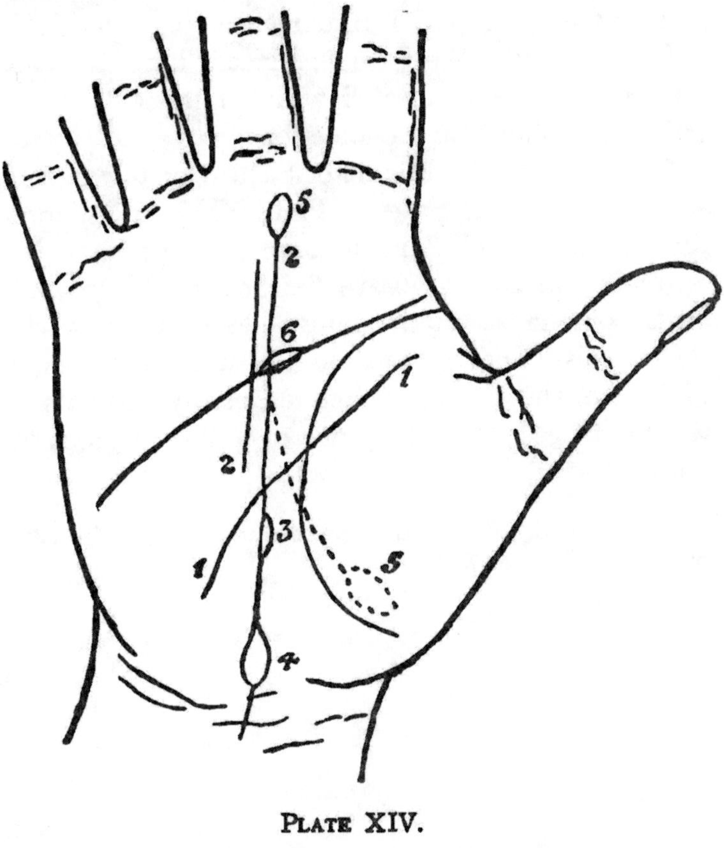

PLATE XIV.

THE LINE OF DESTINY, ISLANDS, AND OTHER SIGNS.

An island, when found on a woman's hand connecting the Fate Line with the Mount of Venus, is an almost certain indication of her seduction (5, Plate XIV.).

An island in any part of the Plain of Mars indicates a period of great difficulty, loss in one's career, and in consequence, generally loss of money (3, Plate XIV.).

An Island on the Fate and Head Lines together means loss also, but more brought on by the person's own stupidity or lack of intelligence (6, Plate XIV.).

An island over the Fate and Heart Lines indicates loss and trouble connected with affairs of the heart or brought about by the affections.

An island on the Mount of Saturn or towards the end of the Line of Fate (5, Plate XIV.) foreshadows that the career will finish in poverty and despair.[1]

When the Line of Fate finishes suddenly with a cross, some great fatality may be expected, but when the cross is found on the Fate Line and on the Mount of Saturn, the ending of such a Destiny will be some terrible tragedy, generally one of public disgrace and public death.

[1] For more details concerning the meaning of "islands" in general, *see* Chapter XV.

CHAPTER VI

THE LINE OF THE SUN

THE Line of the Sun, which is otherwise called the Line of Success or the Line of Brilliancy (1–1, Plate XV.), is one of the most important marks on the hand to consider.

It has in its symbolism almost the same significance as the Sun itself has to the Earth.

Without this line the life has no happiness, no sunshine, as it were, and even the greatest talents lie in darkness and do not produce their fruit.

Amateurs, in looking at hands, often make the greatest mistakes in seeing what appears to be "a good Line of Fate," and in consequence rush off and predict great success and fortune, whereas, as I explained in the preceding chapter, a Fate Line unaccompanied by the Line of Sun may simply mean a fatalistic life full of sorrow and darkness.

The quality that the Line of Sun denotes is, what is generally called "luck"; with a well-marked Sun Line even a poor Line of Head promises more success, and it is the same with the Line of Fate.

People with the Sun Line appear to have more magnetism, more influence over others. They more easily secure recognition, reward, riches, and honours.

They also have a happier and brighter disposition,

and this has naturally a great deal to do with what is called success.

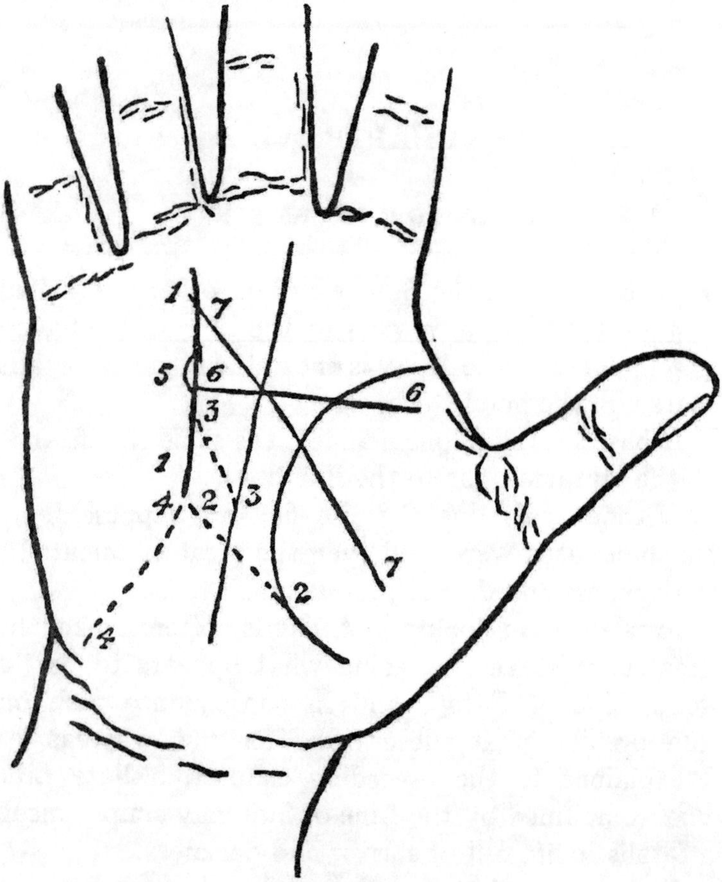

PLATE XV.

THE LINE OF SUN AND ITS MODIFICATIONS.

From whatever date in the hand the Line of Sun appears, things become brighter, more prosperous and important. The Line of the Sun may rise from the following positions:

From the Line of Life, the Line of Fate, the Plain of

Mars, the Mount of the Moon, the Line of Head, and from the Line of Heart, or it may only appear as a small line on its own Mount.

Rising from the Line of Life (2–2, Plate XV.), it promises success from whatever the life is that is led, but not from "luck."

From the Line of Fate (3–3, Plate XV.), it is a sure sign of recognition for the career adopted, but brought about by the personal effort of the subject.

From the Plain of Mars, and not connected with the other lines, it foretells success after difficulties.

From the Mount of the Moon (4–4, Plate XV.), success is more a matter due to the caprice of others. It is more changeable and uncertain and is by no means such a sure sign of riches or solid position. It is more the sign of success as a public favourite, and is, often found in the hands of those who depend on the public for their livelihood, such as actors and actresses, singers, and certain classes of artists, speakers, clergymen, etc. For all such professions it is, however, fortunate, and an extremely lucky sign to have, as it promises in all cases luck, brilliancy, and recognition in the world.

Rising from the Line of Head, the Sun Line gives success from the mental efforts and qualities, but not until after the middle of life is past. It is found on the hands of brain workers, students of some particular branch of study, writers, scientists, etc.

From the Line of Heart, success will come late in life in some way depending on, or through, the affections. In such cases it generally promises a very happy marriage late in life, but it is always a certain sign of eventual ease, happiness, and worldly comfort.

Marked only on its own Mount, the Line of Sun promises happiness and success, but so late in life as to make it hardly worth having.

When the third finger—called the finger of the Sun—is much longer than the first with the Line of Sun well marked, the gambling instincts will be much in evidence. Nearly all successful gamblers for money have these two indications.

When, however, the third finger is equal to the second, the love of amassing wealth will be the dominant passion of the life.

When the third finger is extremely long and twisted or crooked, the person will endeavour to obtain money at any cost. This malformation is much seen in the hands of thieves or criminals who are likely to commit any crime for the sake of money. Note—if the Line of Head is very high on the palm, and more especially if it rises upwards at the end (3-3, Plate III.), these evil qualities will be still more accentuated.

When a hand is found to be artistic in its shape, with pointed fingers or long and narrow, the Line of Sun on such a formation promises rather success and brilliancy in Art, on the Stage, or in Public Singing, than in anything else.

The real musician's hand, such as the composer's or player's, is however rarely a long, thin-shaped hand, because such persons must have a more scientific nature. This quality is not found with those who possess the long, slender, very artistic-shaped hand, who depend more on their emotional temperament than on scientific study for their foundation.

On extremely long, thin hands, those that belong to what is called the Psychic Type,[1] the Line of Sun

[1] *See* Types of Hands, Part II., page 123.

has very little meaning except that of temperament, such persons being too idealistic to care for either wealth, position, or worldly success. They have as a rule, simply bright, happy, sunny dispositions if this line is marked on their hands, and they go through life as in a dream, and their dreams are to them the only things that matter.

A curious characteristic, however, and one that has not been noticed by other writers on this subject, is, that on all hands where the Sun Line is seen, the nature of such people is much more sensitive to environment than that of those persons who do not possess this Line. For this reason the Line has been considered a sign of the artistic nature. But what is known as the "artistic nature" may show itself only in the love of beautiful things, harmony of surroundings, and such like; whereas the people who do not possess any mark of the Sun Line, seldom even notice their surroundings and would live equally happy in the most squalid homes. They would not trouble whether their curtains were black, green, yellow, or some fearful conglomeration of all three.

When many lines are found on the Mount of the Sun, they show also the artistic nature, but one where the multiplicity of aims and ideas will prevent any real success.

Two or three Sun Lines, when running parallel and evenly together, are good and indicate success in two or three different lines of work; but one good, straight, clear line is the best sign to have.

An "island" on any part of the Line of the Sun destroys the position and success promised, but only during the period where the island appears (5, Plate XV.). In nearly all cases it denotes public scandal, and when very clearly marked a *cause célèbre* or something of that sort.

All opposition lines, viz., those that cross over from the thumb side of the hand, and especially those from the Mount of Mars or from its direction, are bad (6–6 Plate XV.). If these opposition lines pass through, cut, or interfere with the Line of Sun in any way, they denote the jealousy or interference of people against one.

Curiously enough, these opposition lines from the Mount of Mars relate to the interference of members of the same sex as the subject; while, if they come from the Mount of Venus, they relate to the opposite sex of the individual on whose hand they appear (7–7, Plate XV.).

A "star" found on the Line of Sun is one of the luckiest and most fortunate signs to have.

A "square" is a sign of preservation against the attacks of enemies or efforts to assail one's position.

A "cross" is an unfortunate sign, and denotes difficulties and annoyance, but only relating to one's name or position.

On a "hollow hand," the Line of Sun loses all power, and its good promises are never fulfilled.

The complete absence of the Line of Sun on an otherwise well-marked hand, indicates that no matter how clever or talented these people may be, the recognition of the world will be difficult or even impossible to gain. In other words, their life will remain in darkness; people will not see their work and the "Sun of Success" will never dawn on their pathway of labour.

CHAPTER VII

THE LINE OF HEART AS INDICATING THE AFFECTIONATE AND EMOTIONAL NATURE

THE Line of Heart is that Line which runs across the hand under the fingers and generally rises under the base of the first, and runs off the side of the hand under the base of the fourth or little finger (1–1, Plate XVI.).

The Line of Heart relates purely to the affectionate disposition, in fact, to the mental side of the love nature of the subject. It should be borne in mind that, by lying as it does on that part of the hand above the Line of Head, it is consequently on the portion of the hand that relates to mental characteristics and not to the physical.

The Line of Heart should be deep, clear, and well coloured. It may arise from the extreme outside of the Mount of Jupiter (2, Plate XVI.), from the centre of this Mount, from the space between the first and second fingers (3, Plate XVI.), from the face of the Mount of Saturn (4, Plate XVI.), or from directly under this Mount (5, Plate XVI.).

From the outside of the Mount of Jupiter, it denotes the blind enthusiast in affection, a man or woman who places his or her ideal of love so high that neither fault nor failing is seen in the being worshipped. With these people their pride in the object of their affection is beyond all reason, and all such extremists as a rule suffer terribly through their affections.

From the centre of the Mount of Jupiter, the Heart

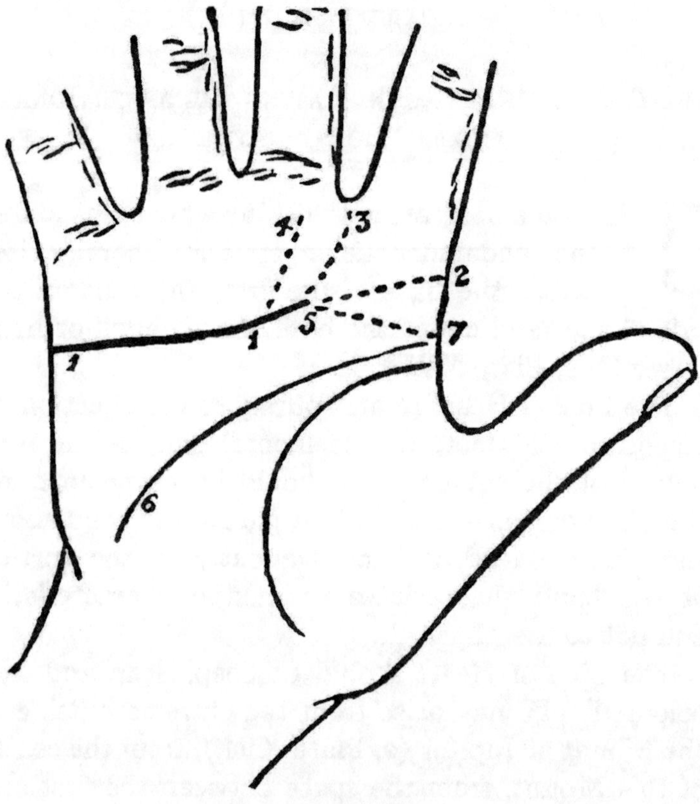

PLATE XVI.

THE LINE OF HEART AND ITS VARIATIONS.

Line gives more moderation, but also great ideality, and is one of the best of the variations of this Line that we are about to consider.

People with such a Heart Line are firm and reliable in their affections, they have an unusually high code of honour and morality. They are ambitious that the person they live with be great, noble, and successful. They seldom marry beneath their station in life, and they have fewer love affairs than any other class.

If they once really love, they love for ever. They do not believe in second marriages, and the divorce courts are seldom troubled with their presence.

The Heart Line rising from between the first and second fingers, gives a calmer but a very deep nature in all matters of the affections (3, Plate XVI.).

These people seem to strike the happy medium between the ideality and pride given by Jupiter, and the more selfish love nature given when the line rises from Saturn.

They are not very demonstrative when in love, but they are capable of the very greatest sacrifices for those they care for. They do not expect the person on whom they bestow their affection to be a god or a goddess.

When the Line of Heart rises on the Mount of Saturn the subject will be rather selfish in all questions of affection (4, Plate XVI.). These people are not self-sacrificing, like the previous type. They are inclined to be cynical, reserved, undemonstrative but very insistent in trying to gain the person they want. They will let nothing stand in their way, but once they have obtained their object they show little tenderness or devotion.

They are very unforgiving if they discover any lapses on the part of their partner, but as they are "a law unto themselves," they close their eyes to their own shortcomings.

The Line of Heart that rises from under the base of the Mount of Saturn (5, Plate XVI.), exhibits all the foregoing characteristics, but in a much more intensified form. Such persons live for themselves, and care little whether those around them are happy or not.

The shorter the Line of Heart is on the Hand, the less the higher sentiments of the affection make themselves manifest.

When the Line of Heart is found in excess, namely, extremely long—it denotes a terrible tendency toward jealousy (2, Plate XVI.), and this is alarmingly increased if the Line of Head on the same hand is very sloping towards the Mount of the Moon (6, Plate XVI.). In such a case the imagination will run away with itself where jealousy is concerned.

When the Line of Heart is found curving downward at the base of the Mount of Jupiter (7, Plate XVI.), it tells of a strange fatality in that person, of meeting with great disappointment in love, and even with those they trust in friendship. He seems to lack perception, in knowing whom to love. His affections are nearly always misplaced or never returned.

These people have, however, as a rule, wonderfully kind, affectionate dispositions. They have little pride about whom they love and they generally marry beneath their station in life.

A Line of Heart made up like a chain, or by a crowd of little lines running into it, denotes flirtations and inconstancy in the love nature, and seldom has any lasting affection.

A Line of Heart from Saturn in holes or links like a chain, especially when it is broad, denotes an absolute contempt for the subject's opposite sex. It is one of the signs of mental degeneration as far as love is concerned.

When this Line is pale and broad, without any depth, it denotes a nature *blasé* and indifferent with no depth of affection.

When very low down on the hand, almost touching the Line of Head, the heart will always interfere with the affairs of the head.

When it lies very high on the hand and the space is narrowed only by the Head Line being abnormally high and out of its place, it indicates the reverse of the above, and that the affairs of the heart are ruled by the head. Such persons are extremely calculating in all matters of love.

When only one deep, straight line is found across the hand from side to side, the two lines both Head and Heart appear to blend together. This denotes an intensely self-concentrated nature. If such a subject loves, he unites with it all the forces of his mind, and if he put his mind on any subject, he throws his whole heart and soul into whatever it may be (Plate VI.).

These people are also terribly head-strong and self-willed in all they do. They do not seem to know what fear means in any sense—they are dangerous lovers and husbands to trifle with, for they will stop at nothing if their blood is once roused.

They are also dangerous to themselves. They rush blindly into danger, and they usually meet with terrible accidents and injuries, and very often suffer a violent death (*see* also page 29).

When the Line of Heart commences with a fork, one branch on Jupiter and the other between the first and second fingers, it is an excellent sign of a well-balanced, happy, affectionate disposition, and a good promise of great happiness in all matters of affection.

When the Line of Heart is very thin and with no branches, it denotes coldness and want of heart.

When there is no Line of Heart whatever, it is a sign of a cold-blooded, unemotional nature. Such people can, however, be brutally sensual and especially so if the Mount of Venus is high (*see* Mounts, page 140).

A broken Heart Line is a certain sign that some terrible tragedy in the affections will at some time or other overwhelm the subject.

It may not often be found nowadays, but I have seen it in some few cases, and these persons never recovered the loss of the loved one or ever had love in their lives again.

CHAPTER VIII

SIGNS RELATING TO MARRIAGE

WHAT is called the Line of Marriage is that mark or marks, as the case may be, found on the side of the Mount under the fourth finger (1, Plate XVII.).

I will first proceed to give all the details possible about these lines, and then call my reader's attention to the other marks on the hand that qualify these Lines of Marriage, and further add a wealth of information regarding them.

The Line, or Lines, of Marriage may be found as very short marks almost on the very side of the hand, or they may appear as quite long lines rising from the side of the hand into the face of the Mount of Mercury, or, in some cases, going farther still into the hand itself.

Only the clearly formed lines relate to marriage, the short ones to deep affection, or marriage contemplated, but never entered into (2, Plate XVII.).

When the deep line is found lying close to the line of Heart, the marriage will take place early in life, but the other marks I am going to explain later will give more accurate dates as to when the event will occur.

For a happy marriage the lines on the Mount of

Mercury should be straight and clear, without breaks or irregularities of any kind (1, Plate XVII.).

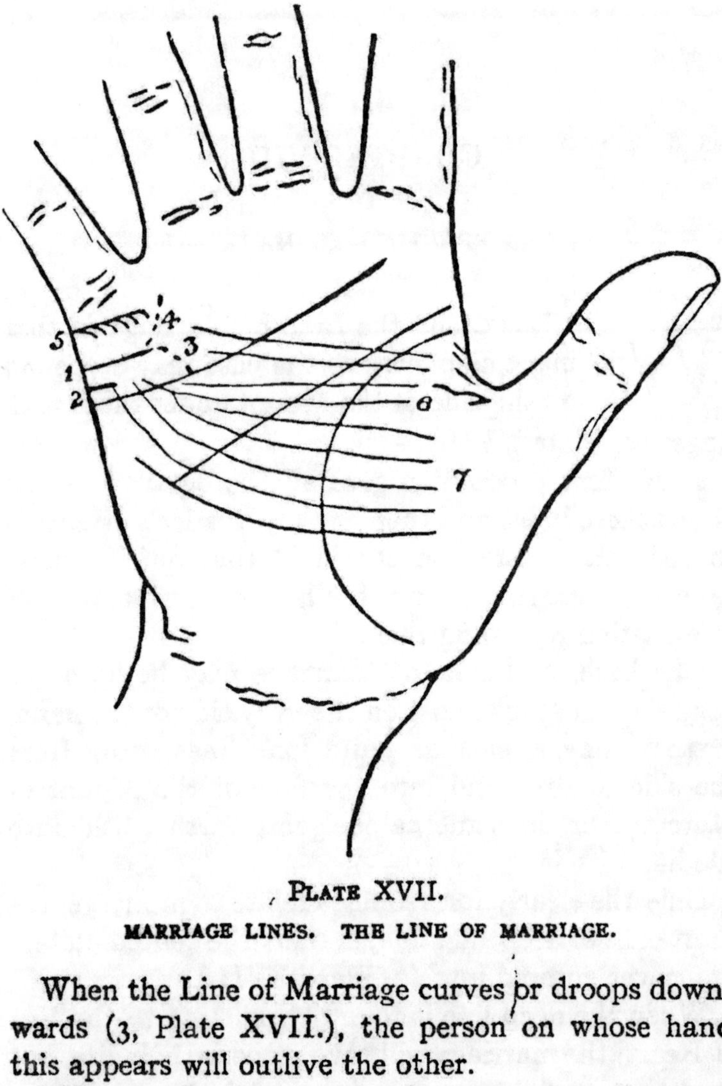

PLATE XVII.

MARRIAGE LINES. THE LINE OF MARRIAGE.

When the Line of Marriage curves or droops downwards (3, Plate XVII.), the person on whose hand this appears will outlive the other.

When the line turns upward in the reverse direction, the possessor is not likely ever to marry (4, Plate XVII.).

When the line is clear and distinct, but has a lot of little lines dropping from it, it foreshadows trouble and anxiety in the marriage, but brought on by the delicacy and ill-health of the partner (5, Plate XVII.).

When the line has a curve at the end, and if a cross or line be found cutting into this curve (2, Plate XVIII.), the partner will die by accident or a sudden illness of some kind. But when the Marriage Line ends in a long, gradual curve into the Heart Line, the death of the partner will come about by gradual ill-health or illness of a very long duration.

When the line has an "island" at the beginning, then the marriage will be for a long time delayed, and the two persons will be much separated at the commencement of their married life.

When the "island" is found about the middle of the Marriage Line, some great trouble and separation will take place about the middle of the married life (3, Plate XVIII.).

When the "island" is found towards the end of the line, the marriage will most probably end in trouble and separation one from the other.

When the Line of Marriage divides into the form of a fork (4, Plate XVIII.), the two people will live apart from one another, but when the fork turns downwards towards the Line of Heart a legal separation may be anticipated (5, Plate XVIII.).

When this fork is more accentuated, and turns down more into the hand, divorce may be expected, and especially so if one end of this fork stretches across the hand in the direction of the Plain of Mars, or the Mount of Mars (5, Plate XVIII.).

In many cases a fine line may be found crossing the entire palm, from the Marriage Line, and in such a case the greatest animosity and bitterness will enter into the fight for freedom and divorce. In such an example there is never any hope of reconciliation.

When the Line of Marriage is full of little islands, or linked like the loops of a chain, the subject should be warned not to marry at any time, as such a union would be full of the greatest unhappiness and continual separations.

When the line, which is otherwise well marked, appears about the centre to break in two, it forshadows a fatality or break-up in an otherwise happy married life.

When the Line of Marriage itself, or an offshoot from it, goes into the hand, and joins or ascends upward with the Line of Sun, it promises that its possessor will marry some one of great wealth or distinction (6, Plate XVIII.).

When this abovc-mentioned line bends downward and cuts the Line of Sun, it denotes that the person on whose hand it is found will lose his position by the marriage he will make.

When any line from the top of the Mount of Mercury falls down into the Marriage Line, it shows that there will be great obstacles to overcome in whatever marriage the subject enters, but if the Line of Marriage is a good one, then such obstacles will be overcome.

When there is another line much slighter in appearance lying close to the upper side of the Marriage Line, it foretells some influence that will come into the subject's life after marriage.

All lines that cross the hand from the Mount of Mars (6, Plate XVII.), and rise up towards the Line of Marriage denote the interference of people with the marriage. These lines give the date of the interference when they cross the Line of Destiny; they cause quarrels when they come from Mars; from Venus they also denote annoyances, but not of such a vindictive nature (7, Plate XVII.).

INFLUENCE LINES TO THE FATE LINE ON THE MOUNT OF VENUS, AND OTHER SIGNS WHICH ALSO HAVE A MEANING IN CONNECTION WITH MARRIAGE

The student may also get very great help in ascertaining details about the likely marriage of the person whose hands he is examining by the following:

Fine Influence Lines seen joining the Line of Fate (7, Plate XVIII.), relate to persons who come into and affect the Destiny.

If the Line of Influence is very strong where it joins the Fate Line, and if at about the same date a clear Marriage Line is seen on the Mount of Mercury, the date of marriage may be more accurately predicted by the place on the Fate Line where the Influence Line joins it.

A great wealth of detail may also be made out from observing these Influence Lines to the Destiny.

Coming over from the Mount of the Moon; there is always something romantic about the union. The person on whose hand this Line appears will as a rule meet his affinity when travelling or away from his home.

If the Influence Line has an "island" marked on it, the influence will then be a bad one, or, at least, the person will have had some scandal connected with his or her past life (8, Plate XVIII.). If the Line of Fate looks weaker or more uncertain after the union is marked, then such a marriage has not brought good or success to the subject. If, on the contrary, the Line of Fate looks better or stronger after the Influence

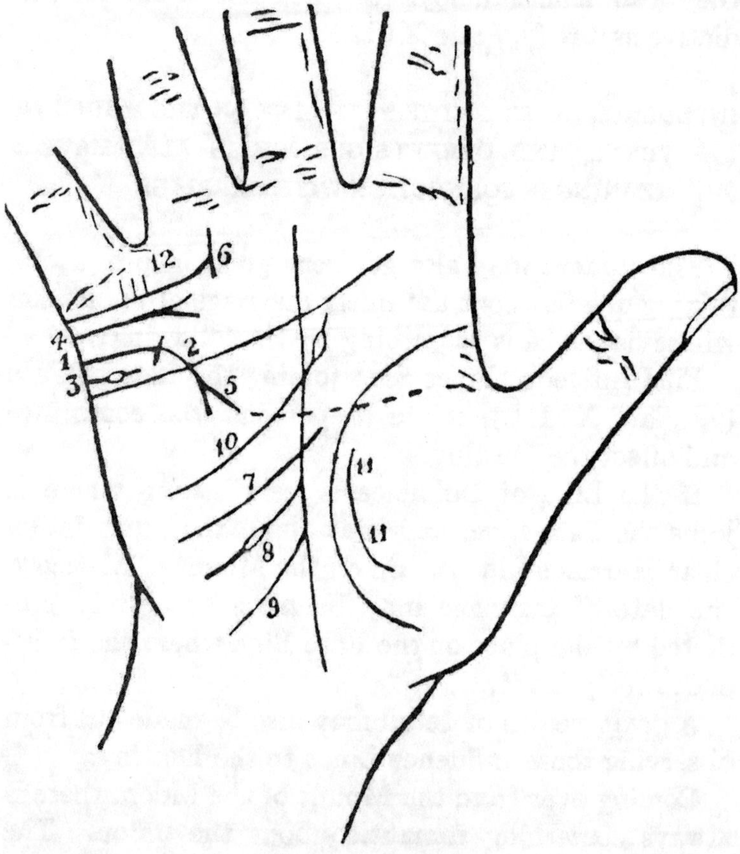

PLATE XVIII.

MARRIAGE LINES AND INFLUENCE LINES WHICH FURTHER HELP IN DENOTING MARRIAGE.

Line has joined it, then this union will prove of advantage to the person whose hand is being examined.

This increase of wealth or power is still more accentuated if at the same time it is observed that a Sun Line has made its appearance.

If the Influence Line should cut through the Fate Line, and appear on the thumb side of it, the affection will seldom last as long, or be so happy (7, Plate XVIII.). If a still wider separation of the Influence Line and the Fate Line appear as these two lines ascend the hand together, the separation of interests and destiny of the two persons will be still more marked as the years proceed.

If an Influence Line approaches close to the Line of Fate, and runs parallel with it for some time but does not join it, some great obstacle will prevent a marriage ever taking place (*see* also page 57).

If an Influence Line terminates in an "island," the influence itself will itself get into trouble, generally disgrace of some character (10, Plate XVIII.).[1]

INFLUENCE LINES ON THE MOUNT OF VENUS

These are fine lines that run parallel with the Line of Life (11–11, Plate XVIII.), but they must not be confounded with the Line of Mars, or "Sister Life Line," which commences higher up nearer the Mount of Mars.

These Venus Influence Lines are more often found with those persons who have what is called the "Venus temperament," or who are intensely emotional and passionate.

When many of such lines are seen, the subject cannot live without love, and will have many "affairs" at the same time.

As such an Influence Line runs parallel with the Life Line, or turns away from it, so it can be judged

[1] For further particulars refer back to chapter on the Line of Destiny, where these Influence Lines are also referred to (page 57).

how long such an influence will last, and with fair accuracy the date when it will occur (for dates *see* page 113).

These Influence Lines, however, never have the same importance or meaning as those previously ascribed to the Line of Fate.

In my large work on this subject, Cheiro's *Language of the Hand*, I have been able to go into still greater detail with regard to all these Influence Lines.

CHAPTER IX

LINES DENOTING CHILDREN, THEIR SEX, AND OTHER MATTERS CONCERNING THEM

THE Lines relating to children are those finely marked upright lines found immediately above the Line of Marriage (12, Plate XVIII.). A very good plan, in trying to see these Lines, is to press this portion of the hand with the tips of the fingers, and then note which of these small lines stand out the most clearly.

Sometimes they are extremely deeply marked, and as a rule much more so on a woman's hand than on a man's. In many cases it is necessary to employ a magnifying glass in order to see them.

Broad and deep lines denote male children, fine and narrow lines, females.

When they appear as straight lines they denote strong healthy children, but when very faint or crooked, the children indicated are always delicate.

When the first part of the little line (taking it upward from the Line of Marriage) is marked with a small "island," such a child will be very delicate in its early life, but if the line appears well marked when the "island" is passed, the probability is that it will grow up strong and healthy. When ending or broken at the "island" the child will never grow up.

When one line stands out very clear and distinct among the others, the child the mark indicates will be more to the parent, and will be more successful than any of the others.

To know the number of children anyone will have, it is necessary to count these lines from the outside of the hand in towards the palm.

A person with the Mount of Venus very flat on the hand, and very poorly developed, is not likely to have any children at all, and this is all the more certain if the first Bracelet is found rising up like an arch into or towards the palm (*see* page 91).

CHAPTER X

THE LINE OF HEALTH OR THE HEPATICA

THERE has been very considerable discussion among students of this subject as to the part of the hand on which the Line of Health (1–1, Plate XIX.) commences.

My own theory, and one that I have proved by over twenty-five years' experience and also watching its growth on the hands of children, is, that it rises at the base of or on the face of the Mount of Mercury, and as it grows across the hand and attacks the Line of Life, it foreshadows the development of illness or germ of disease, which, at the date of its coming in contact with the Line of Life, will reach the climax of its attack.

The Line of Life, it must be remembered, merely relates to the promised length of life from heredity and natural causes, but the Line of Health denotes the effect of the class of life the subject has led. Where these two lines come together, if one is of equal strength to the other, will be the date of death, even though the Line of Life should pass this point and appear to be a much greater length (2, Plate XIX.).

The Line of Mercury, or of Health, relating as it does to the nervous system, and also to the mind (Mercury), lends itself to the supposition that the all-knowing subconscious brain is cognisant, even at an early age, of the force of resistance in the nervous system. It may know how long this force will last,

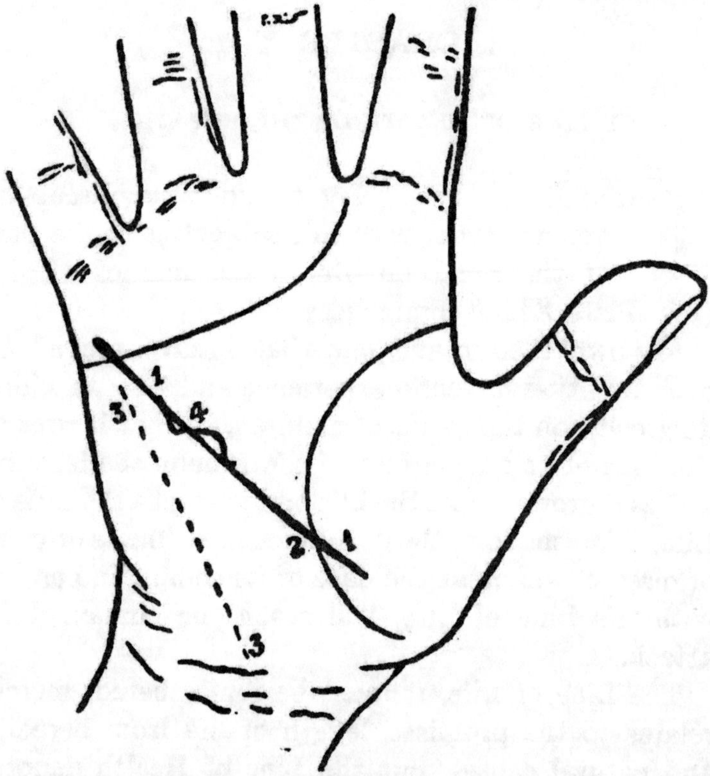

PLATE XIX.

THE LINE OF HEALTH.

when it will be exhausted, and consequently may mark the hand long years in advance.

The Line of Health is one of the lines of the hand most subject to changes. It is the thermometer of the life showing its "rise and fall" as the case may be. I have seen this mysterious line look deep and threatening during the early years of a life, and completely fade away as greater health and strength took possession of the body.

Again, I have often seen it look deeper and more ominous as the wear and tear, especially of the nervous system, began to make itself manifest, or when the subject over-taxed his mental strength.

Further, it is an excellent sign to be without this line altogether. Its absence denotes an extremely robust, strong constitution, and a healthy state of the nervous system.

If a hand has the Line of Health, the best position for it is to lie straight down the hand, and not approach or touch the Line of Life (3–3, Plate XIX.). When found crossing the hand, and touching or throwing branches across to the Line of Life, it foretells that there is some illness at work which is undermining the health.

If it rises and seems like a branch from the Heart Line, especially if both these lines are broad in appearance and with the Health Line running down the palm coming in contact with the Line of Life, it is a certain indication of weakness or disease of the heart.

The student should always observe the kind of nails there are on the hand when thinking out the diseases indicated by the Line of Health.[1]

When the finger nails are short, without moons, and round, and the Line of Health is strongly marked, he may be sure that nervous weak action of the heart is decidedly threatened.

When the nails are long and almond-shaped, there is danger of weakness and delicacy of the lungs. With the same shape of nails, and with islands in the

[1] *See* Chapter on Nails, page 136.

upper part of the Health Line (4, Plate XIX.), consumption of the lungs and tuberculosis will make itself manifest.

When the nails are very flat, and especially shell-shaped (*see* Plate V., Part II.), and the Line of Health is deeply marked, paralysis and the worst forms of nerve diseases are threatening the subject.

When this line is very red in small spots, especially when pressed, rheumatic fever is indicated.

When twisted, irregular, and yellowish in colour, the subject will suffer from biliousness and liver complaints.

When found heavily marked, and only joining the Heart and Head Lines together, it foreshadows brain-fever, especially when any islands are marked on the Line of Head.

The Line of Health, running straight down the hand but not touching the Line of Life, indicates that though the constitution may not be robust, it is wiry, and there is great reserve resistance to disease.

In connection with the examination of the Line of Health, the student must always look for other indications to the rest of the lines of the hand, more especially to the Line of Life and Line of Head. For instance, when the Line of Life looks very chained and weak, the Health Line on a hand will naturally increase the danger of delicate health; and when found with a Line of Head full of little islands, or like a chain, such a Health Line more clearly foreshadows brain disease, severe headaches, etc.

By a study of this line the most valuable warnings may be given of approaching ill-health. Whether persons will follow the warnings or not is a question. My experience is that they do not and will not, and therefore, whatever is indicated will most probably come to pass.

Providence places many signposts and warnings in our paths, but human nature is either too blind or too self-confident to notice them until it is too late.

CHAPTER XI

THE GIRDLE OF VENUS, THE RING OF SATURN, AND THE BRACELETS

THESE marks are classed among the minor lines of the hands, but they often have a significance that is of the greatest importance.

The Girdle of Venus is that broken or sometimes unbroken kind of semi-circular line that is found rising from the base of the first finger to the base of the fourth (1–1, Plate XX.).

I have not in my experience found this mark to indicate the gross sensuality that is so often ascribed to it by other writers. It should be remembered that the hand is divided by the Line of Head, as it were, *into two hemispheres, the lower and the upper.*

The lower relates to the physical or more animal side of the nature, and the upper to the intellectual. Following this arrangement, it is only reasonable to assume that this mark under consideration, viz., the Girdle of Venus, relates more to the mental side of the symbolism of the Venus nature.

I have found that persons with this sign are more mentally sensual than physically so. They love to read or write books on the subject of the "sex problem;" but they are not inclined to put their theories and ideas into practice, at least with their own lives.

The qualities, however, that this mark represents are much more active and dangerous when this Girdle

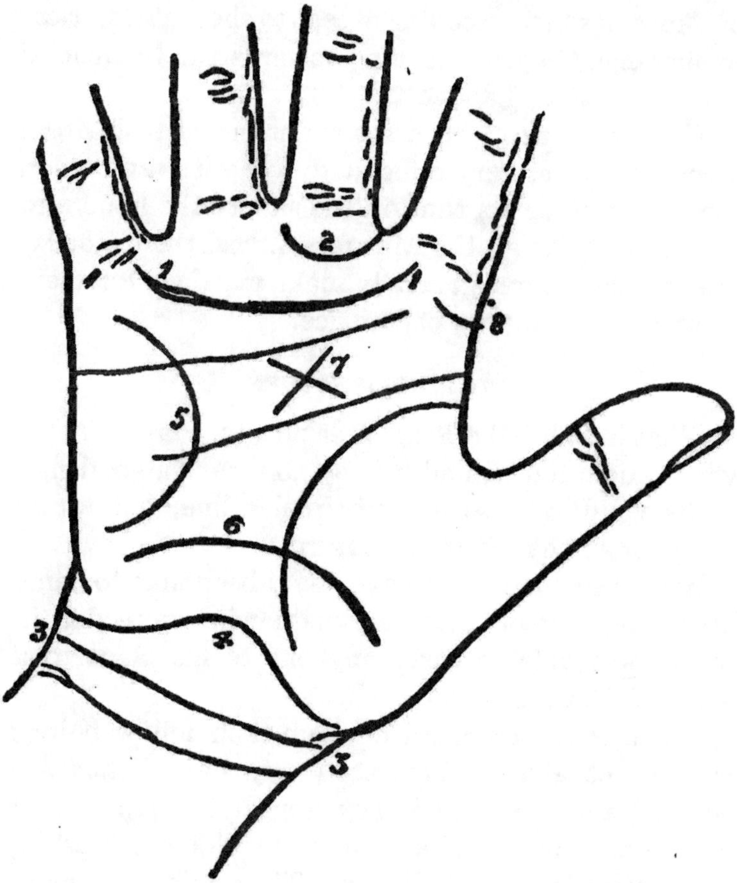

PLATE XX.

THE GIRDLE OF VENUS, THE RING OF SATURN, THE THREE BRACELETS, THE LINE OF INTUITION AND THE VIA LASCIVA.

forms itself from the Mount of Saturn to that of Mercury. The imaginings of such people are then morbid and unhealthy.

To those who study Astrology, the inference that

I draw from the connection of these two parts of the hand will become clear and reasonable.

When broken or made up of little pieces, the Girdle of Venus has little meaning except to show a hysterical temperament, with a leaning towards the tendencies I have mentioned above.

These persons in all cases suffer enormously from moods, they are very difficult to live with, and when the Girdle of Venus runs off the side of the hand and passes out through the Marriage Lines, their moody, changeable natures generally make marriage for them an unusually unhappy experience.

THE RING OF SATURN

What is called the Ring of Saturn (2, Plate XX.) is very seldom found, and it is by no means a good sign to have. It is also a semi-circular line, but found lying across the Mount of Saturn.

In all my experience I have never been able to come across any person with this mark who succeeded in life or was able to carry any one of his plans to a successful termination.

These people seem cut off from their fellow beings in some peculiar and extraordinary way. They are isolated and alone, and they appear to realise their lonely position keenly. They are gloomy, morbid, and Saturnine in character. They seldom marry, and when they do it is always a ghastly failure.

They are terribly obstinate and headstrong in all their actions, they resent the least advice or interference in their plans. Their lives generally close in suffering, poverty, or by some sinister tragedy or fatality.

It is the most unfortunate mark ever to find.

THE BRACELETS

The Bracelets (3-3, Plate XX.) are of very little importance except to throw light on certain points of health. There are supposed to be three of these lines or bracelets at the wrist, which were called by the Greeks the Bracelets of Health, Wealth, and Happiness.

It is certainly very seldom that they can be found together, for experience in life does not give much hope that these three much-sought-after possessions can ever be found together on this side of the grave.

Delving back into the ancient legends of Greece, we find one very significant point in reference to the first bracelet, the one nearest the palm, which represents Health.

It appears that at one period of the ancient Greek civilisation all women had to come to the priest at their Temple to have their hands examined before they were allowed to marry. If the priest found this first Bracelet out of its place and rising up into the hand in the shape of an arch (4, Plate XX.), he would not allow the woman possessing this sign to be married under any circumstance, the idea being that it represented some internal malformation that would prevent her bringing children into the world. In such cases these women were made Vestal Virgins in the temples. Perhaps the old Greek Priest was right in his idea, for if this first Bracelet is found rising into the hand in the form of an arch, both men and women possessing it are delicate internally, and especially so in matters relating to sex.

CHAPTER XII

THE LINE OF INTUITION AND THE VIA LASCIVA

THE Line of Intuition (5, Plate XX.) is seldom found on other types of hand than those of the Philosophic, the Conic, and the Psychic, but it is sometimes found on the Spatulate.

It takes more or less the formation of a semi-circle from the face of the Mount of Mercury to that of the Mount of the Moon, or may be found on the Mount of the Moon alone. It must not be confounded with the Hepatica, or Line of Health, but is found as a distinct mark in itself.

It denotes an extra highly-strung sensitive temperament, also presentiments, inspiration, clairvoyance of the highest kind, clear vivid dreams which often come to pass, intuition as to how things should be done, and very often manifests itself in inspired speaking and writing of the loftiest character.

It is much more often found on women's hands than on men's, although many cases have come under my notice of its being unusually clearly marked on some men's hands. In each case the possessor of it had most remarkable powers and unusual faculties, as well as the gift of intuition, even concerning purely mundane subjects that in an ordinary state they knew nothing whatever about.

I use the words "ordinary state" advisably here, because such people are not always in the condition of mind when these strange faculties may be employed. Several of these men were absolutely uneducated, and yet at times, when thrown into an inspired state, they were able to explain the most intricate problems with the greatest accuracy. If asked, however, from where they obtained their knowledge, they were only able to reply that "it came to them" when in certain moods.

One man I knew well had such remarkable dreams of coming events that he was able to warn many people weeks and months in advance of dangers that lay before them, and his warnings in many cases saved life.

With all people who were gifted in this way I have noticed that they completely lost their strange powers the moment they indulged in alcohol of any kind.

THE VIA LASCIVA

This is a strange mark (6, Plate XX.) which takes the form also somewhat of a semi-circle, but in this case it connects the Mount of the Moon with that of Venus, or it may simply run off the hand from the lower part of the Mount of Luna into the wrist.

The first-mentioned formation indicates unbridled sensuality and passion, and where it cuts through the Line of Life it indicates death, but one usually brought about in connection with the licentiousness that it denotes.

This Line running from the Mount of the Moon into the wrist denotes the most sensual dreams, desires, and imaginings, but, unlike the other class, it is usually only dangerous to the person on whose hand it is found.

In both cases there is generally a tendency towards the taking of drugs such as opium, morphine, especially when the hand is noted to be soft, full, and flabby. With a firm hard palm the subject usually indulges in excessive drinking fits, and when under drink seems to have no control whatever.

If the Line of Head is found weak-looking, full of islands and descending downwards on the Mount of the Moon, insanity or the worst form of degeneracy will sooner or later destroy the whole character and career.

CHAPTER XIII

"LA CROIX MYSTIQUE", THE RING OF SOLOMON

WHAT is called "La Croix Mystique" is found in the quadrangle of the hand between the Lines of Heart and Head (7, Plate XX.). It is more usually found in the centre of this part of the hand, but it may be also found nearer the one side of the quadrangle or the other.

This mark denotes a natural gift or talent for mysticism and occultism of all kinds.

When placed nearer Jupiter, it denotes the employment of these studies more to gratify the subject's own pride or ambition than the following out of such things for their own sake.

When it is in the centre of the quadrangle, across the Line of Fate, or immediately under the Mount of Saturn, such studies become more of a religion or are followed for their own worth and the influence and truth of occultism will play a leading rôle in the whole career. Most likely the possessor of this mark will follow it as a profession, or will crystallise his researches into the form of books.

When this mark lies lower down in the quadrangle, nearer to the Mount of the Moon, the subject will study some form of occultism more from a superstitious standpoint than any other. None the less, he will be likely to succeed in doing so, and influence other people through his studies, and with this latter form he will be more likely to write beautiful mystic poetry with the prophetic note running through it very strongly.

THE RING OF SOLOMON

The Ring of Solomon is also one of these strange marks of mysticism and occultism, but in this latter case, owing probably to the qualities signified by the Mount of Jupiter, its possessor will aim at having the power of a master or an adept in such subjects (8, Plate, XX.).

CHAPTER XIV

TRAVELS, VOYAGES AND ACCIDENTS

TRAVELS and voyages may be seen on the hand by the little lines that leave the Line of Life and bend over towards the Mount of the Moon and also by the lines found on this Mount (2, Plate XXI.).

When these fine lines of travel are seen on the Line of Life, by referring to the map showing dates (Plate XXVI.), it may be possible to obtain a very clear idea of when these travels take place.

When, however, the Line of Life itself divides, and one branch of it leans over towards or on to the Mount of the Moon (1, Plate XXI.), it denotes that the entire life will be full of change and travel. In such a case it will not be possible, except by the use of some gift such as clairvoyance, to tell accurately in advance the dates of voyages that will be undertaken.

If the Line of Life apparently leaves its ordinary course and sweeps over to the Mount of the Moon, the life will be one continual round of travel. The person will settle nowhere, and the end of the life in such a case will take place in some land far distant from the place of birth.

If the Line of Life has no line or branch leaving it and going in an opposite direction, but keeps to the form of a semi-circle round the Mount of Venus, then such a life will be remarkably free from change and travel, and the person will remain all his life in the land of his birth (3–3, Plate XXI.).

When a travel Line from the Line of Life ends in a small cross the journey undertaken will end in disappointment (4, Plate XXI.).

When the Line ends in a square, there will be great danger to the subject on such a journey, but he will escape, as the square is a sign of preservation from danger.

When the Line ends in an island, the journey will end in loss (5, Plate XXI.).

When the Travel Line crosses over near or on to the Mount of the Moon and ends in a fork or a circle, there will be great danger of the subject losing his life in undertaking such a journey.

There is always more danger in travelling on water when the subject is found to be born in the following dates:

(1) Between the 21st of June and the 21st of July.

(2) The 21st of October and the 21st of November.

(3) Between the 21st of February and the 21st of March.

There is more likelihood of danger from collision of trains and accidents on land when the subject is born between:

(1) The 21st of April and 21st of May.

(2) The 21st of August and the 21st of September.

(3) The 21st of December and the 21st of January.

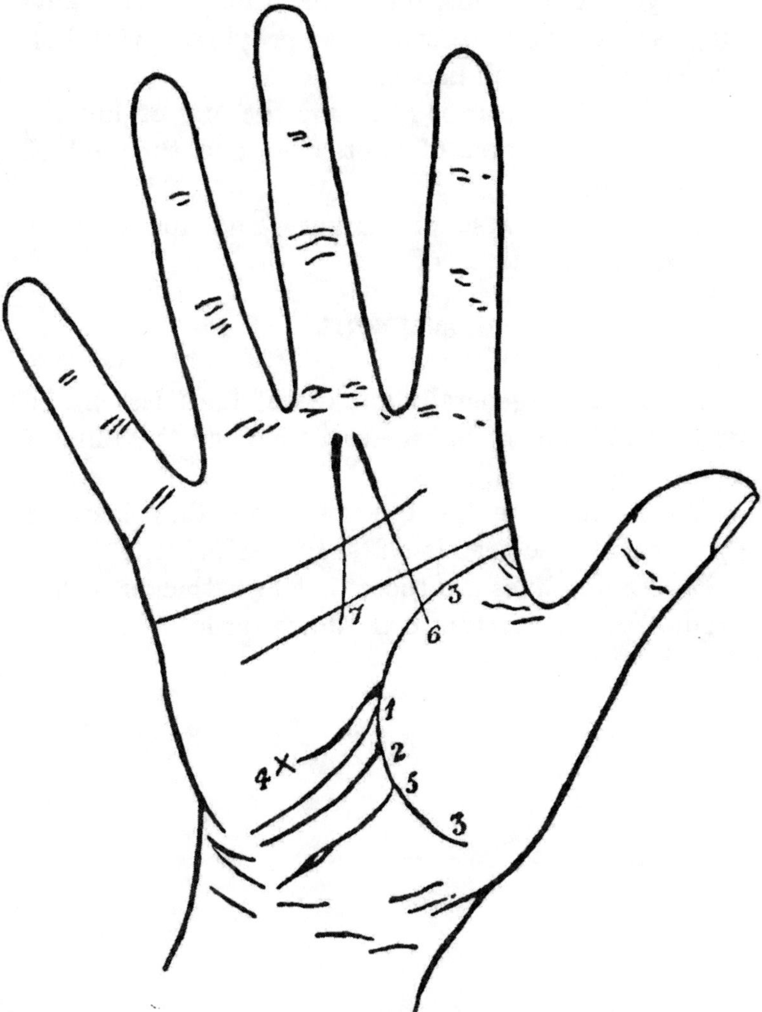

PLATE XXI.

TRAVELS, VOYAGES, ACCIDENTS AND DESCENDING LINES FROM THE MOUNTS.

Danger from storms, tornadoes, thunder and lightning, is more likely to occur when people are travelling whose birthdays fall between:

(1) The 21st of May and the 21st of June.

(2) The 21st of September and the 21st of October.

(3) The 21st of January and the 21st of February.

ACCIDENTS

Accidents are generally marked by lines descending from the Mount of Saturn and touching the Line of Life (6, Plate XXI.).

When falling on the Line of Head, they increase the danger to the head itself (7, Plate XXI.).

Descending lines are those that look thicker on the Mount and taper as they come downwards.

CHAPTER XV

THE ISLAND, THE CIRCLE, THE SPOT, AND THE GRILLE

THE Island is never a fortunate sign. Wherever it makes its appearance, it reduces the promise of the Line or Mount on which it may be found.

On the Line of Life it shows delicacy or illness at that particular date where it appears (1, Plate XXII.).

On the Line of Head, weakness of the brain, danger of brain illness (2, Plate XXII.).

On the Line of Heart, weakness of the heart (3, Plate XXII.), and especially so when under the Mount of the Sun.

On the Line of Fate, heavy loss in worldly matters, worry, and anxiety about the subject's destiny (4, Plate XXII.).

On the Line of Sun, loss of position and generally by some scandal (5, Plate XXII.).

On the Line of Health, serious illness (6, Plate XXII.); if on the upper part of the Line and with small round finger-nails, throat and bronchial troubles. With long nails, delicacy of the lungs and chest. With short nails without moons, bad circulation and weak action of the heart; and with very flat nails, nerve diseases and paralysis (*see* Nails, page 137).

Lower down on the Line of Health on the Mount of

the Moon, it indicates a grave tendency towards kidney and bladder troubles (7, Plate XXII.).

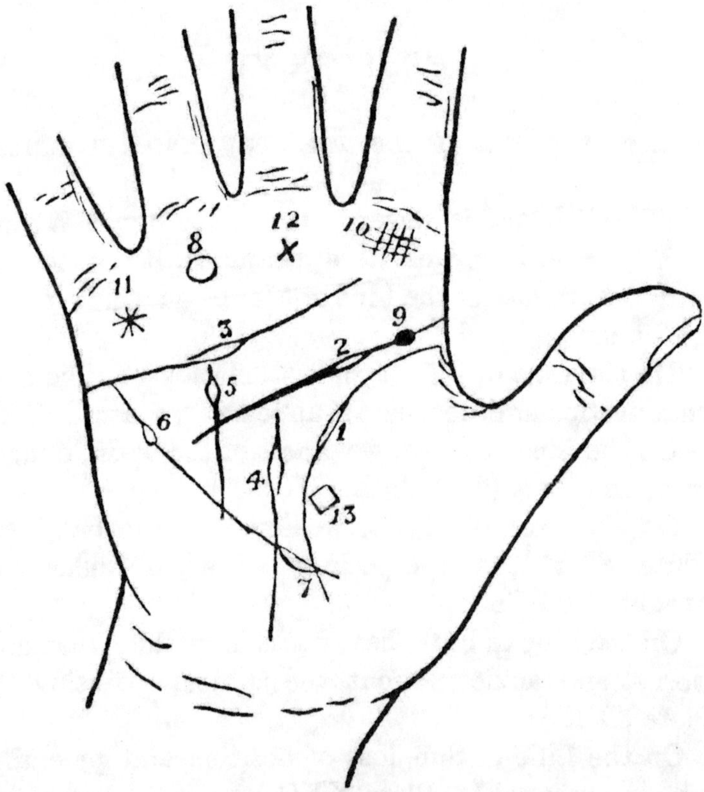

PLATE XXII.

THE ISLAND, THE CIRCLE, THE SPOT, THE GRILLE, THE STAR, THE SQUARE.

Any Line that forms itself into an island or that runs into one, is a bad sign for that Line or particular part of the hand on which it is found. An island on any of the Mounts weakens the qualities of what the Mount expresses.

THE CIRCLE

On the Mount of the Sun the Circle is favourable (8, Plate XXII.) in all other positions it is unfavourable. On the Mount of the Moon it threatens death from drowning.

THE SPOT

The Spot is a sign of temporary arrest of the qualities of any Line on which it may be found.

On the Line of Head, shock or injury. (9, Plate XXII.)

On the Line of Life, sudden illness.

On the Line of Health, fever.

On all the other Lines it appears to have less significance.

THE GRILLE

The Grille (10, Plate XXII.) is very often seen on the Mounts of the Hand. It denotes difficulties and obstacles in connection with whatever the Mount represents, and a lack of success in whatever quality or talent the Mount symbolises.

CHAPTER XVI

THE STAR, THE CROSS, THE SQUARE

THE Star (11, Plate XXII.) is with only one exception a most fortunate mark to possess.

On the Mount of Jupiter, the Star promises added honour, power, and position.

On the Mount of Sun, it gives riches and glory, but generally associated with a public life.

On the Mount of Mercury, unusual success in commerce, business, science, or great eloquence, according to other indications of the hand. (11, Plate XXII.)

On the Mount of Mars under Jupiter, great distinction and celebrity in martial life or in some one decisive battle, which gives renown to the rest of the career, like a Wellington at Waterloo.

On the Mount of Mars under Mercury, it gives honour won by the mentality fighting the battle of life (*see* Mounts, page 144).

On the Mount of the Moon it is a sign of great celebrity arising from the qualities of this Mount, viz., through the imagination or inventive faculties.

On the Mount of Venus the Star on the centre of this Mount is also a sign of success, but in relation to animal magnetism and sensuality it gives extraordinary success with the opposite sex.

On the Mount of Saturn it is the one unfavourable

sign of this particular mark, and on this Mount it gives distinction, but one to be dreaded. Such a person

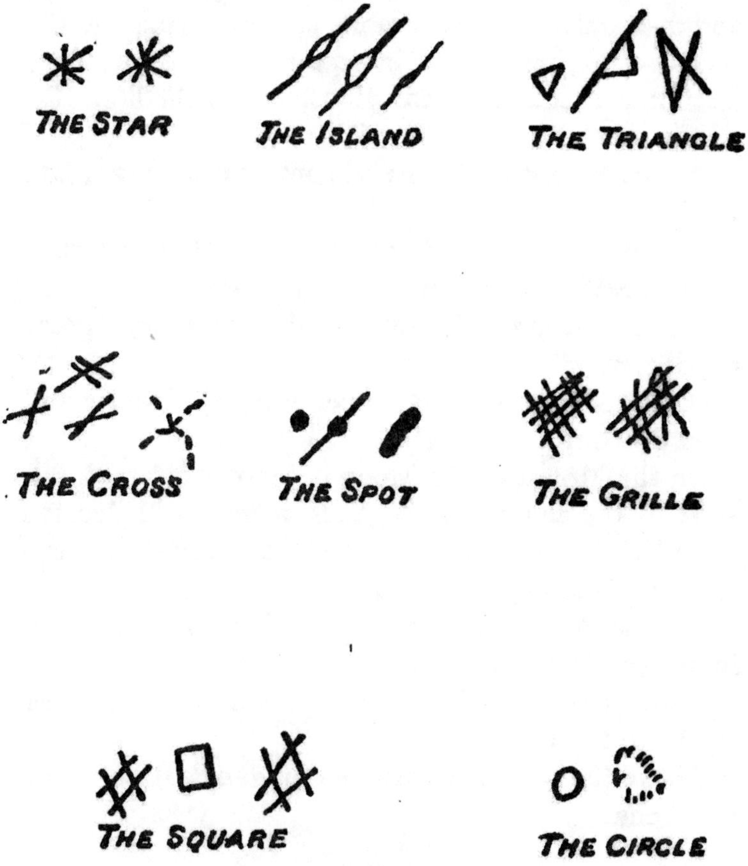

PLATE XXIII.

MINOR MARKS AND SIGNS.

will be the plaything of destiny, a man cast for some terrible part in the tragedy of life. Such a man's life will end in some terrible disaster, but one which will cause his name to be on everyone's lips. A king perhaps, but one crowned by doom.

THE CROSS

This sign is the direct opposite to the preceding sign, and has only one favourable position, viz., on the Mount of Jupiter where it indicates some extraordinary fortunate affection which will come into the life. On all the other Mounts it is evil.

On the Mount of Saturn, violent death. (12, Plate XXII.)

On the Mount of Sun, disappointment in riches.

On the Mount of Mercury, dishonesty.

On the Mount of Mars (under Mercury) great opposition.

On the Mount of Mars (under Jupiter) violence and even death from quarrels.

On the Mount of the Moon it denotes a fatal influence to the imagination. Such a man will deceive himself. When low down on this Mount it foreshadows death by drowning.

On the Mount of Venus it indicates some fatal influence of the affections.

Above the Line of Head it foretells an accident or injury to the head.

Above the Line of Heart, the sudden death of some loved one.

THE SQUARE

The Square (13, Plate XXII.) is usually called the Mark of Preservation. It shows escape from dangers at that particular moment where it appears.

When on the Line of Life it means preservation from death. (13, Plate XXII.)

On the Line of Fate, preservation from loss, and so on with each quality represented by the different lines.

CHAPTER XVII

DIFFERENT CLASSES OF LINES

THE lines on the palm should be clearly marked, a good pink or reddish colour, and they should be free from breaks, crosses, holes or irregularities of all kinds.

When very pale in colour they show lack of force and loss of energy, and often poor health.

When extremely red they indicate excessive energy and a rather violent disposition.

When yellow in colour they denote a tendency to biliousness and liver complaints, and tell in consequence of a melancholy morose nature.

Forked lines are generally good and increase the quality of the special indication. When at the end of the Line of Head, the fork gives more of what is called a dual mentality and less power of concentration on any one subject. (Plate XXIV.)

Spots on a Line weaken it and arrest its growth.

Tasselled Lines (Plate XXIV.) are not good signs. They weaken any indication the line itself denotes, and at the end of a Life Line they foreshadow loss of all nervous energy.

Wavy Lines (Plate XXIV.) show uncertainty, lack of decision and want of force.

Broken Lines (Plate XXIV.) destroy the meaning of

the line at the particular place where the break appears, but if one line ends above the other, the break is not so bad and the quality of the line will be continued.

Sister Lines (Plate XXIV.) increase or double the

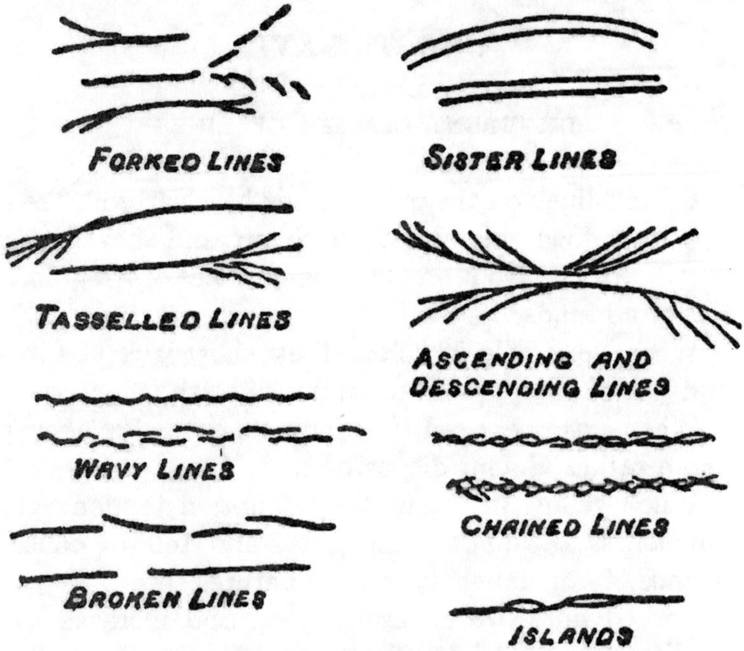

PLATE XXIV.

MINOR MARKS AND SIGNS.

power of any line, and when lying close together at the Line of Head, they give it great power and promise.

Islands (Plate XXIV.) are always evil and denote weakness or failure of the Line or Mount on which they may be found.

Ascending Lines (Plate XXIV.) are good from any line from which they spring. From the Line of Life they denote increased energy wherever they make their appearance. If they run up to any particular Mount or part of the hand, they show that the increased effort or energy will be in that particular direction.

Descending Lines (Plate XXIV.) are the reverse and mean loss of power.

Chained Lines show lack of force or fixity of purpose. (Plate XXIV.).

When the entire hand is covered with a network of small lines, it denotes a highly nervous disposition and usually great mental worry and lack of decision.

RIGHT AND LEFT HANDS

Both the hands should be examined together to see if they accord. When they do, the indication of whatever the mark is, is more decided.

When something is marked on the left hand and not on the right, the tendency will be in the nature, but unless it is also marked on the right hand it will never bear fruit or come to any result. When the two hands are exactly alike, it denotes that the subject has not developed in any way from what heredity or Nature gave to him.

It must be remembered that we use the left side of the brain more than we do the right, and the nerves cross and go to the right hand. Consequently, it is this hand which denotes the developed or active brain, the left only giving the natural tendencies or inclinations.

To be scientific and accurate the student of this subject must always keep this rule before his mind and not be led away in his judgment by some "marvellously good line" that the subject may proudly call his attention to in the left hand, for such a mark will have no actual result unless it is also found on the right hand.

CHAPTER XVIII

THE GREAT TRIANGLE AND THE QUADRANGLE

THE Great Triangle is formed by the lines of Head, Life, and Health (Plate XXV.). The larger this triangle is, the better will be the health, for the reason that the Line of Health will be further removed from the Life Line. The views of life will also be broader and the field of action as it were less limited.

When the upper angle (made by the Head and Life Lines) is acute, the subject will be more nervous, timid, and sensitive.

THE QUADRANGLE

The Quadrangle, as its name implies, is that space lying between the Lines of Head and Heart. (Plate XXV.)

To be well marked, it should be even in shape and not narrow at either end.

When marked in this way it denotes balance of judgment, level-headedness in all things, and is a most excellent sign to have.

It represents man's disposition or mental attitude towards his fellow men. When extremely narrow it indicates narrowness of views and bigotry in regard to religion.

When excessively wide, it denotes a lack of judgment in all things and too much looseness of views for one's good.

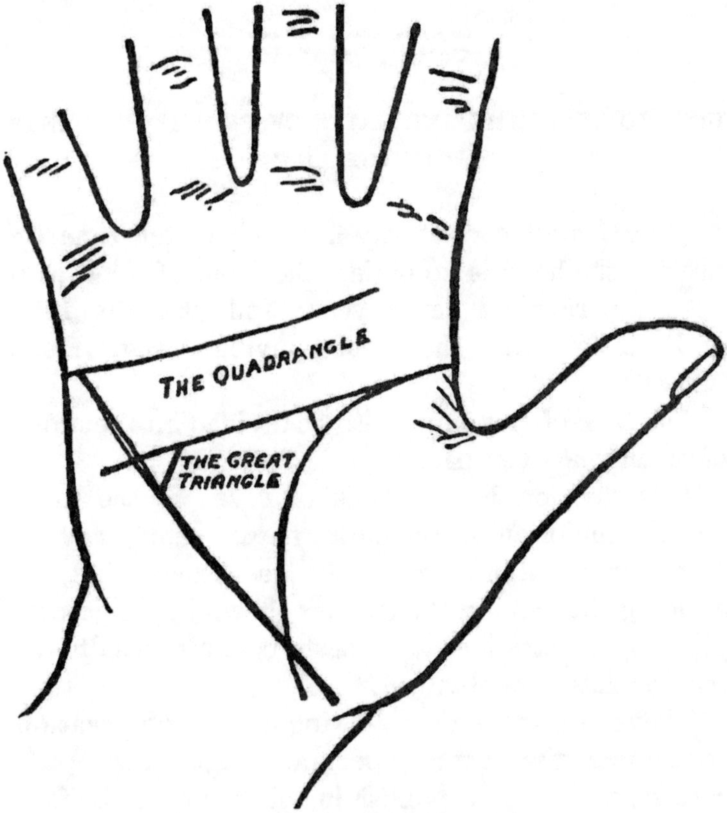

PLATE XXV.

THE GREAT TRIANGLE AND THE QUADRANGLE.

CHAPTER XIX

HOW TO TELL TIME AND DATES OF PRINCIPAL EVENTS IN THE LIFE

THE most correct way in which to tell time by the hand is to divide the Line of Life into periods of seven years, and also the Line of Fate, following the accompanying design (Plate XXVI.).

The Line of Head may also be divided into sections of seven years (*see* page 25).

This division into periods of seven is the most natural one of all, as the entire nature changes every seven years. Long experience has proved that, by dividing the hand in the manner shown in the accompanying illustration, the best possible results as regards dates are obtained.

I have also made the following curious observation concerning the most important years in people's careers, which I now publish in this work for the first time.

People born on the 1st, 10th, 19th, and 28th of any month, and especially in the months of July, August, and January, will find the following years of their lives the most eventful:

1st, 7th, 10th, 16th, 19th, 28th, 34th, 37th, 43d, 46th, 52d, 55th, 61st, and 70th.

Those born on the 2d, 11th, 20th, and 29th of any month, but more especially in July, August, and

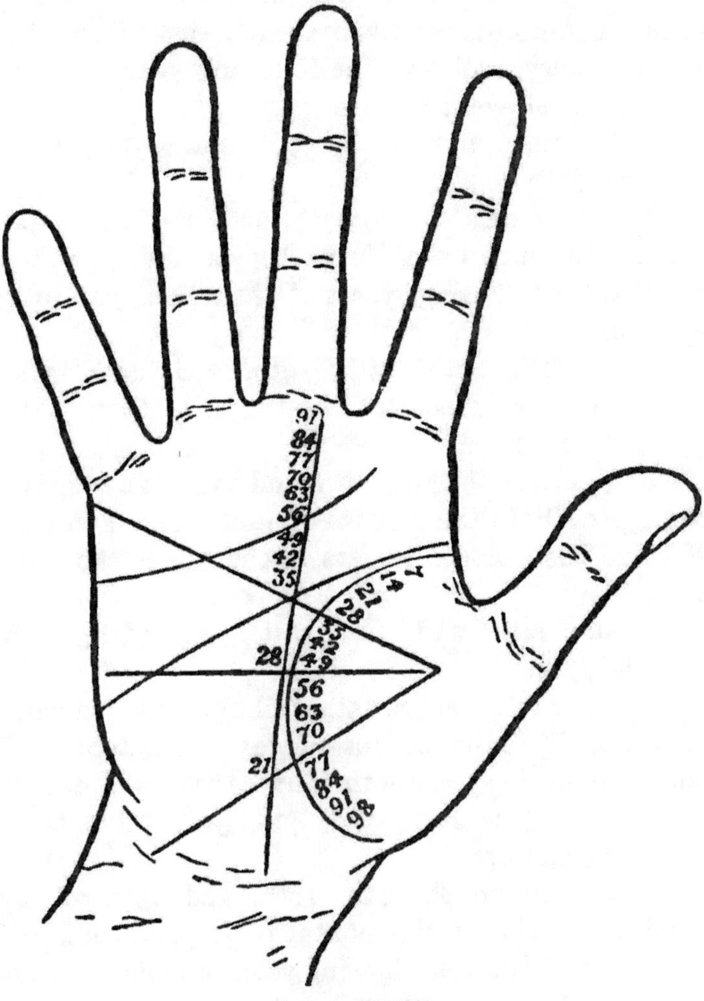

PLATE XXVI.

TIME AND DATES OF PRINCIPAL EVENTS.

January, will find the following years of their lives the most eventful:

2d, 7th, 11th, 16th, 20th, 25th, 29th, 34th, 38th, 43d, 47th, 52d, 56th, and 70th.

Those born on the 3d, 12th, 21st, and 30th of any month, but more especially in the months of December and February, will find the following years of their lives the most eventful:

3d, 12th, 21st, 30th, 39th, 48th, 57th, 66th, and 75th.

Those born on the 4th, 13th, 22d, and 31st, especially in the months of July, August, and January, will find the followings years of their lives the most eventful:

1st, 4th, 10th, 13th, 19th, 22d, 28th, 31st, 37th, 40th, 46th, 49th, 55th, 58th, 64th, 67th, 73d, and 76th.

Those born on the 5th, 14th, and 23d of any month, but especially in the months of June and September, will find the following years of their lives the most eventful:

5th, 14th, 23d, 32d, 41st, 50th, 59th, 68th, and 77th.

Those born on the 6th, 15th, and 24th of any month, but especially in the months of May and October, will find the following years of their lives the most eventful:

6th, 15th, 24th, 33d, 42d, 51st, 60th, 69th, 78th, and 87th.

Those born on the 7th, 16th, and 25th of any month, especially in the months of July, August, and January, will find the following years of their lives the most eventful:

2d, 7th, 11th, 16th, 20th, 25th, 29th, 34th, 38th, 43d, 47th, 56th, 61st, 65th, 70th, 74th, and 79th.

Those born on the 8th, 17th, and 26th of any month,

but more especially in the months of January, February, July, and August, will find the following years of their lives the most eventful:

8th, 17th, 26th, 35th, 44th, 53d, 62d, 71st, and 80th.

Those born on the 9th, 18th, and 27th of any month, but more especially in the months of April, October, and November, will find the following years of their lives the most eventful:

9th, 18th, 27th, 36th, 45th, 54th, 63d, 72d, and 81st.

This curious system it will be seen has embraced every day of every month that people can be born on. It is based on a strange law of periodicity that after years of study I have found extremely accurate and wonderful in its meaning.

PART II—CHEIROGNOMY

OR

THE SCIENCE OF INTERPRETING THE SHAPE OF HANDS

CHAPTER I

THE STUDY OF THE SHAPE OF THE HAND

WE now leave the domain of what must be considered Palmistry, the study of the Lines of the Palm—or Cheiromancy, as it was called by the Greeks from the word χείρ, the hand, and proceed to consider the meanings that can be derived from the shapes of the hands, fingers, etc., which is called Cheirognomy.

These two studies may be taken up separately, but by a knowledge of both the student will be doubly armed, especially in the reading of character.

To a judge of horseflesh the limbs of the horse give him such a fund of information as to the animals' breed, training, etc., that it enables him to draw conclusions that he could not otherwise obtain.

In the same way the shape of the hand gives an enormous wealth of information as to breed and peculiarities of human beings.

In a book of this nature I shall be able to give only

the leading traits denoted by each type, but if readers wish to carry out this study further, I must refer them to my larger works on the subject, in which the shapes of the hands are described in the fullest detail.

The most casual observation of character as shown by the formation of hands will soon convince any person of the value of this study. Even in itself it possesses the most far-reaching possibilities in helping to a clear understanding of the difference that exists in races, their various blends of types, that have now spread themselves by intermarriage and travel over the surface of the earth.

For example, the difference in the shape of the hands of the French and German or the French and English races would convince any thinking person that temperament and disposition are indeed largely indicated by the shape of the hand itself.

It is even a remarkable thing that though work and exercise may enlarge and broaden the hand, yet the type to which it belongs is never destroyed, but can be easily detected by anyone who has made a study of such matters.

The Seven Types or Shapes of Hands are as follows:

(1) The Elementary—or lowest type.
(2) The Square—or the useful hand.
(3) The Spatulate—or nervous active type.
(4) The Philosophic—or jointed hand.
(5) The Conic—or the artistic type.
(6) The Psychic—or the idealistic hand.
(7) The Mixed Hand.

THE SEVEN TYPES OF HANDS

THE ELEMENTARY

As its name implies, the Elementary is the lowest type of all. It is just a little above the brute creation. This type is extremely short (Plate I., Part II.), thick set and brutal-looking. In passing I must draw the reader's attention to the fact that the shorter and thicker the hand is, the nearer the person is to the animal.

In examining this type one can therefore only expect to find it the expression of all that is coarse, brutal, and animal.

People having such hands naturally have very little mental development or ability. They are found engaged in occupations requiring only unskilled labour and the very lowest even of that.

They are violent in temper, and have little or no control over their passions or their anger. They are coarse in their ideas, possess little or no sentiment, no imagination or feeling, and it has been found that even the nerve system of such types is more or less in a state of non-development. They do not feel pain as the higher types of humanity feel it, and have little ambition except to eat, drink, and sleep.

Note.—The thumb is extremely short and low-set with the Elementary type.

THE SQUARE TYPE

The Square type (Plate I., Part II.,) is so designated on account of the palm being like a square in shape, or at least nearly so. Such a hand in fact "looks square."

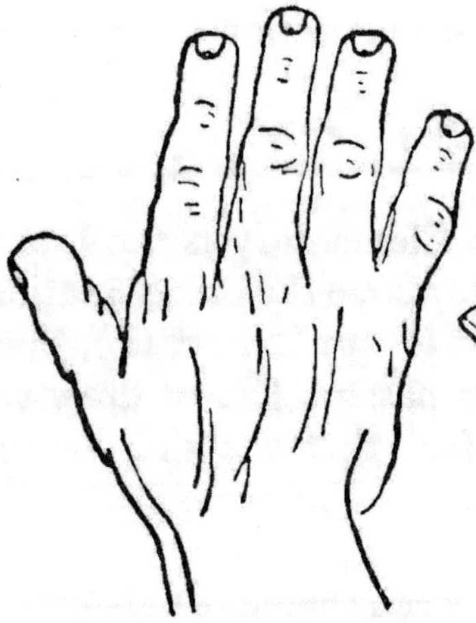

FIG. 1—THE ELEMENTARY HAND.

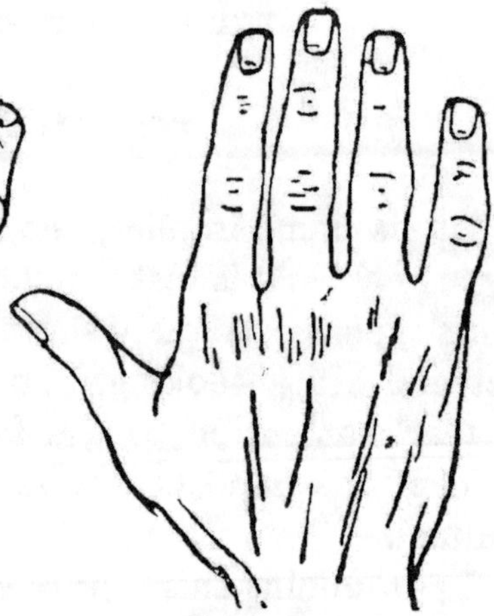

FIG. 2—THE SQUARE OR USEFUL HAND.

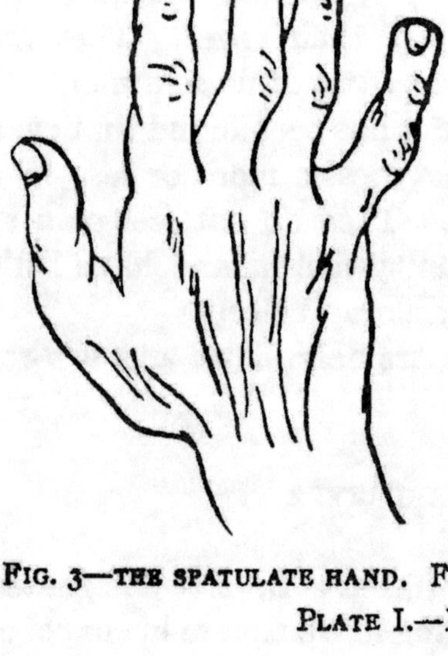

FIG. 3—THE SPATULATE HAND.

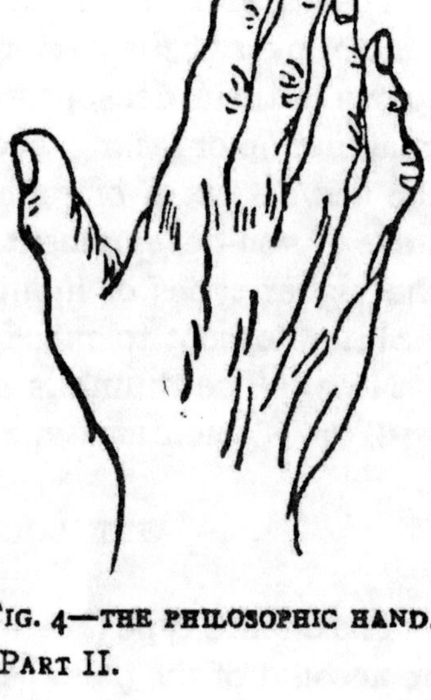

FIG. 4—THE PHILOSOPHIC HAND.

PLATE I.—PART II.

It is rather straight or even at the wrist, at the base of the fingers, and also at the sides. The fingers themselves also have a "square-cut" appearance. The thumb is, however, nearly always long, well-shaped, and set high on the palm, and stands well out from the palm.

The Square Hand is also called the practical or useful hand. People who possess this type are essentially practical, logical, and rather materialistic. They belong to the earth and the things of the earth. They have little imagination or idealism, they are solid, serious workers, methodical and painstaking in all they do. They believe in things only by proof and by their reason. They are often religious and even superstitious, but more from habit than from anything else.

They are determined and obstinate, especially if their thumbs are long and the first joint stiff.[1]

They succeed in all lines of work that do not require imagination or the creative faculties, and as business men, lawyers, doctors, scientists, they do extremely well, and are generally to be found in such callings.

THE SPATULATE HAND

The Spatulate or active nervous type (Plate I., Part II.) is usually crooked or irregular looking, with large tips or pads at the ends of the fingers, rather like the spatula chemists use and from which peculiarity this type gets its name. The people who possess this type are in fact always "pounding" at something. They are full of untiring energy, enormous workers in

[1] *See* Chapter on Thumbs, page 127.

everything they take up, and generally remarkable for their originality.

They are not built on the hard set square lines of the former type. These persons have enormous imagination, their creative faculties largely developed. They are inventive, unconventional, emotional, demonstrative, and in fact the complete opposite in character to the class who possesses the square type of hand.

The Spatulate type has also the palm irregular in shape. It may be wider at the base of the fingers than at the wrist, or it may be found *vice versa*.

In the first case they are then more practical in their work and views and less impulsive. With the larger development at the wrist, they are more carried away with their impulses, hasty and impetuous in temper, speech, and action.

THE PHILOSOPHIC HAND

The Philosophic Hand (Plate I., Part II.) received this name from the Greek φιλος—love, and σοφια—wisdom. When the Greeks made a study of hands they noticed that all those persons who possessed this type had a bent for philosophy in their blood that nothing could eradicate.

The Philosophic Hand is long, bony, and angular with knotty joints, and is as a general rule fairly thin. People with this type of hand are always studious. They are great readers and usually have a strong tendency towards literature. They love sedentary work, and have a somewhat lonely, ascetic disposition. Perhaps on account of this quality they are very often found in church-life, orlargely associated with religious movements. The monks of old, I mean those who

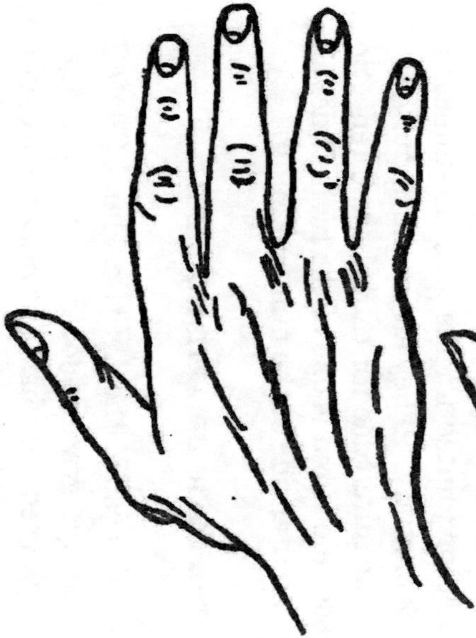

FIG. 1.—THE CONIC OR ARTISTIC HAND.

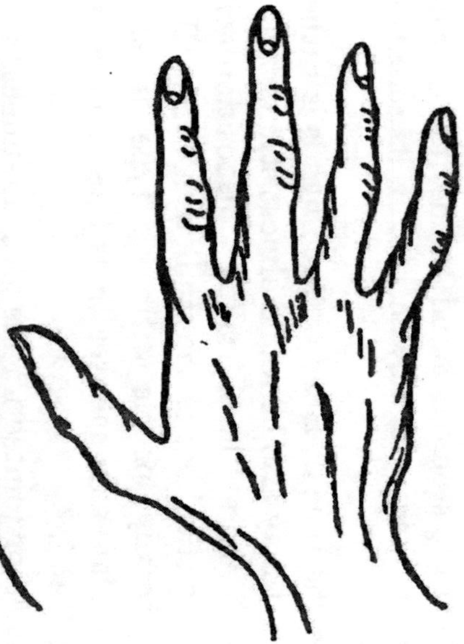

FIG. 2.—THE PSYCHIC OR IDEALISTIC HAND.

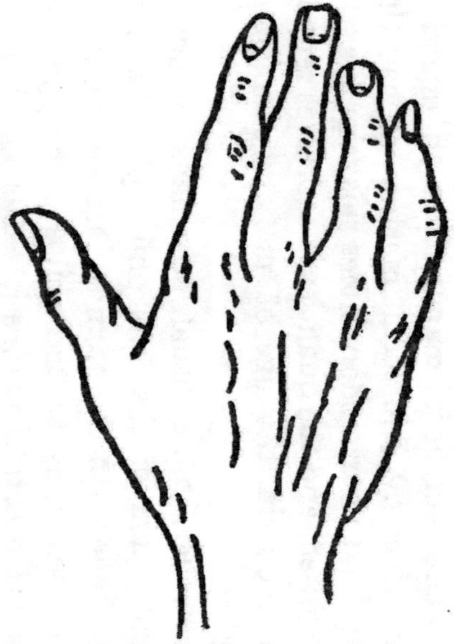

FIG. 3.—THE MIXED HAND.

PLATE II.—PART II.

compiled those wonderful manuscripts on doctrine, science, art, alchemy, and occult matters, all had this class of hand. In our modern times this type may be easily recognised, and the qualities it expresses remain the same even in the age of money-getting and machinery.

It is, however, more usual nowadays to find a slight modification of the true philosophic hand in that of the hand with the palm square and with the fingers only belonging to the philosophic type. In such cases the practical nature is a basis or foundation on which the studious mind builds its theories, its religion, its literary achievements, or its scientific researches.

As a rule the Line of Head on such hands is rather sloping, but it may also be found almost straight, and when it is, a more "level-headed" disposition will make more practical use of the studious nature. But speaking generally, people with this type of hand rarely accumulate as much wealth as those possessing the Square Hand.

The knotted or jointed fingers give carefulness and detail in work or study. They arrest the impulse of the brain, and so acquire time for thought and reflection.

The Philosophic Hand is one of the highest developments of the mental side of the human family.

THE CONIC OR ARTISTIC HAND

The Conic, also called the Artistic, Hand (Plate II., Part II.), is always graceful looking, with the fingers tapering and pointed. It has, not only on account of its appearance but also because of the qualities it represents, been called the Artistic Hand.

Its possessor may not always paint pictures or design beautiful things, but he will have the emotional, artistic temperament, which loves beautiful surroundings, and is most sensitive to colour, music, and all the fine arts. It largely depends on the kind of Head Line and the will power shown by it, to determine whether its owner will develop the natural artistic temperament that he or she possesses.

Such hands being generally full, fleshy, or soft, there is always a decidedly pronounced indolence in the nature which, if not overcome, combats the hard work necessary to achieve any real result. All very emotional people have more or less the characteristics of this type, but great numbers simply squander their time in the appreciation of art, rather than in making the effort in themselves to create it.

The harder and firmer this type of hand is, the more likely it is to find that its possessor will really make something out of his artistic temperament.

THE PSYCHIC OR IDEALISTIC HAND

This type (Plate II., Part II.), may in many ways be considered as the highest development of the hand on the purely mental plane, but from a worldly standpoint it is the least successful of all. Its possessors live in a world of dreams and ideals. They know little or nothing about the practical or purely material side of existence, and when they have to earn their own bread they gain so little that they usually starve.

These beautiful hands do not appear made for work in any sense. They are also too spiritual and frail to deal blows and hold their own in the battle of life. If they are supported by others, or have money of their own to live on, all may be well, and in such cases they will be likely to develop strange psychic gifts dealing with visions and ideals that some few may hear and understand. But if not, their fate as a rule is a sad one, they will easily be pushed aside by the rougher types of humanity or, in sheer helplessness, take their own lives, and so end the unequal struggle.

In constitution they are seldom strong physically, and consequently they are doubly unfitted for the struggle for existence.

THE MIXED HAND

What is called the "Mixed Hand" (Plate II., Part II.), is an aggregation of all the types, or at least, some of them.

It is very often found having all the fingers different from one another, as for example one pointed, one square, or spatulate, and so on. Or sometimes the palm may be of one type, say spatulate, with all the fingers mixed.

Such persons are always versatility itself, but so changeable in purpose that they rarely succeed in making much out of any talents they may possess. They can generally do a little of everything but nothing well. They can talk on any subject that may crop up, but never impress their listeners with depth of thought on any subject.

It is only when the Line of Head is found on such hands clear and straight that there is a likelihood of these persons developing some one talent out of the versatility that this type gives.

CHAPTER II

THE THUMB

IN the judgment of character by the formation of the Hand, the Thumb is of about the same importance as the nose is to the face. It must be understood to represent the natural Will Power, whereas the Line of Head represents the Mental Will.

In my larger works on this subject I have gone into very deeply the medical reasons why character should be expressed by the Thumb and the extraordinary rôle it has played in civilisation, and also in the various religions of the world.

The Thumb proper represents the three great worlds of ideas, viz., Love, Logic, and Will (Plate VI., Part II.).

Love is represented by the base of the Thumb which is covered on the hand by the Mount of Venus.

Logic is the middle phalange, and Will is the top or nail portion.

When these divisions are found large, the qualities are increased; when small, they play a smaller rôle in the life of the individual.

There are two distinct classes of Thumbs, the supple-jointed and the firm-jointed.

The former of these divisions is the Thumb bending

outwards and supple at the joint underneath the nail (Fig. 2, Plate III.).

This denotes a nature pliable and adaptable to others, very broad-minded, rather unconventional, and not obstinate in its views of life. These characteristics will be increased if the Head Line be found sloping and bending downwards. If, however, the Line of Head be found lying straight across the palm, they are more conventional. The "supple-jointed" thumb also denotes generosity of mind both as regards thought and money. In all ways these people are more extravagant than people who have the straight firm-jointed thumb. In other words they "give more" even in what they think as well as in what they do.

The nearer the Thumb approaches the side of the hand, or the more it looks tied down or cramped to the palm, the more the subject is inclined to grasp or hold. The true miser has always a thumb cramped towards the hand, and the nail phalange as a rule slightly turned in, as if the mind wanted to grab, hold or retain.

The supple-jointed Thumb is more impulsive in its desire to give than is the stiff-jointed class, whereas the latter type demands reflection before he even gives an opinion.

If a favour should be asked of the man with the supple-jointed Thumb, one should remember that he is more inclined to give in on the impulse of the moment, and if one does not press one's point home at once, he is likely first to promise, and later, on reflection, change his mind.

The man with the stiff-jointed Thumb (Fig. 3, Plate III.) on the contrary, is more likely to refuse at first and on reflection to agree to the proposition; but if

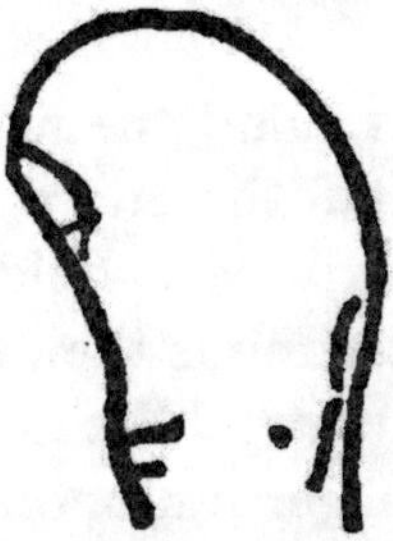

Fig. 1.—The clubbed thumb.

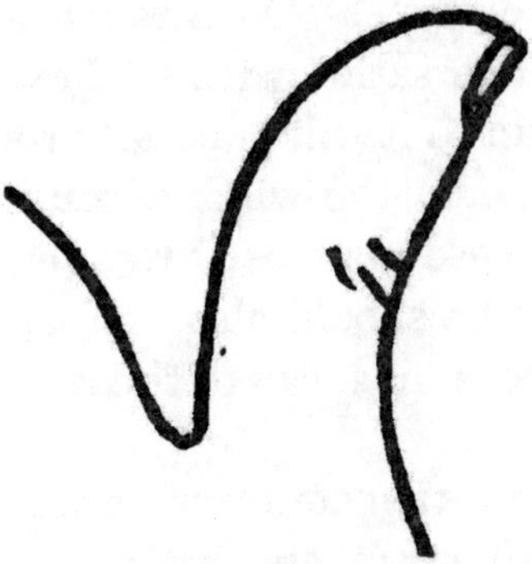

Fig. 2.—The supple-jointed thumb.

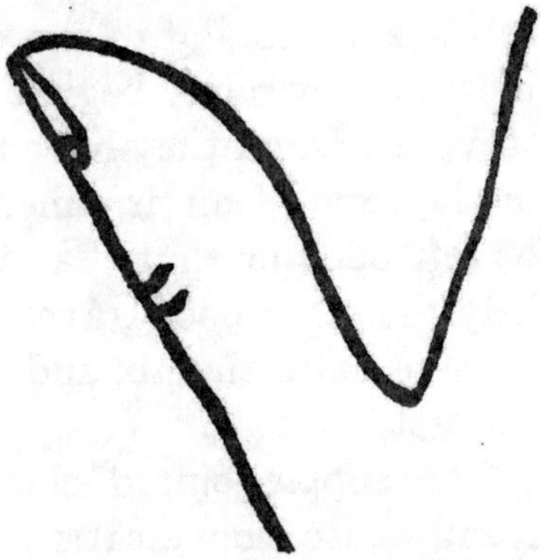

Fig. 3.—The firm-jointed thumb.

Fig. 4.—The waist-like thumb.

Fig. 5.—The straight thumb.

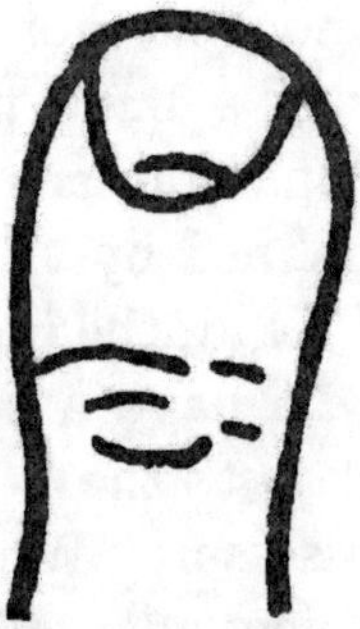

Fig. 6.—The elementary thumb.

Plate III.—Part II.

he does make up his mind, he will stick to his judgment or opinion, and the more he is opposed the more determined he will be to hold to his view.

The firm-jointed thumb is then the outward sign of a more resisting nature, and the longer the first or nail phalange is, the stronger and more powerful the Will force.

These people seldom make friends so easily or rapidly as those belonging to the other type. On a railway journey they rarely begin a conversation with a fellow traveller, and if they have to do so it will generally be in the form of an argument that "the window must be left open or shut," as the case may be. Heaven help the other poor traveller if he should also happen to have a stiff thumb, and oppose his ideas to those of the first.

The supple-jointed class, on the contrary, enter readily into conversation with strangers, and they often make their greatest friends while travelling. They are affable, charming companions, and give in readily to the wishes of others. In fact, this quality inclines to a weakness that should be guarded against. Among all those men and women who take the "easiest way" a large majority will be found to have very supple-jointed thumbs. This, however, will be greatly qualified by the position and appearance of the Line of Head, the indicator of the developed mental Will.

To have a supple lower or middle joint does not relate to the Will but to the phalange of Logic of the possessor. When this second joint is found supple the subject adapts himself to circumstances rather than to persons. He reasons out that he must bend or adapt himself to the conditions or circumstances of the life in which he is placed.

The Clubbed Thumb (Fig. 1, Plate III.), is so called from its being thick like a club. People possessing this class of Thumb belong to the Elementary type as far as Will is concerned. They are brutal and like animals in their unreasonable obstinacy. If they are opposed they fly into ungovernable passions and blind rages. They have no control over themselves, and are liable to go to any extreme of violence or crime during one of their tempers. In fact the clubbed-shaped Thumb has also been designated "the murderer's thumb" on account of so many murderers having been found with this formation.

The possessor of a Clubbed Thumb could not, however, plan out or premeditate a crime, for he would not have the determined Will or power of reason to think it out.

The shorter the Thumb, the nearer the possessor is to the brute in passion and lack of self-control.

The "waist-like" Thumb (Fig. 4, Plate III.), and the "straight" formation (Fig. 5), must also be considered as the opposite of one another in their characteristics, but in this case the difference is in the quality of Logic or Reason. The former will not use or depend much on such things, he will rely, on the contrary, on tact and diplomacy to gain his point or win his way. The second class have little or no tact, but in all matters depend on argument and reason.

The third phalange of the Thumb, which is placed under the designation of Love (Plate VI., Part II.), when found long, denotes more control over the quality of Love or Sensuality; when short and thick-set, the passion or sensual nature is more brutal and animal.

The space at my disposal in this work will not allow

me to go deeper into all the shades of character that can be made out by a study of the Thumb alone, but I think I have said enough to show my readers the great truth in D'Arpentigny's words that "the Thumb individualises the man."

CHAPTER III

THE FINGERS—LENGTH TO ONE ANOTHER

THE SMOOTH AND THE KNOTTY

THE First Finger is called the Finger of Jupiter.
The Second " " " Saturn.
The Third " " " The Sun.
The Fourth " " " Mercury.

The Finger of Jupiter, when long, gives love of power and command over others. When short it denotes dislike of responsibility and lack of ambition.

The Finger of Saturn when long gives prudence, love of solitude and a reserved, studious disposition. When short it denotes frivolity and general lack of seriousness in all things.

The Finger of the Sun when long gives love of the beautiful, desire for celebrity and fame, but when excessively long, the tendency inclines more toward notoriety, risk in speculation, the love of money and gambling. When short it denotes a dislike of all these things.

The Finger of Mercury when long gives mental power, grasp of languages, and power of expression, especially in speech. When short it denotes difficulty in speaking, and in the expression of thoughts. When crooked, with an irregular Head Line, it is an evil sign of the Mentality.

The fingers should be long in proportion to the palm; they then denote greater intellectuality and mental power. When short and stubby looking, the subject is inclined to animalism and gross materialism.

When the fingers lean towards one another, they

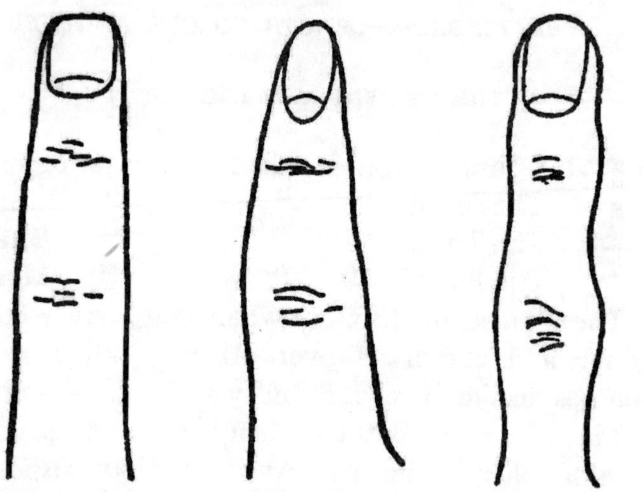

PLATE IV.—PART II.

DIFFERENT SHAPES OF FINGERS.

take after the qualities expressed by the finger towards which they lean.

A wide space between the thumb and first finger denotes independence of will and fearlessness.

When wide between the first and second fingers, independence of thought; between the second and third fingers, independence of circumstances; and wide between the third and fourth fingers, independence of action.

When the fingers are found loose and inclined to

curve backwards, the subject is "open-minded" and quick to grasp ideas or suggestions. They will not, however, have the more methodical stick-at-it quality of those whose fingers are found firm and stiff.

When the fingers are curved inwards, the subject is slower to grasp new ideas, very cautious, and inclined to hold on to what he knows or what he has.

Smooth-jointed fingers are more impulsive than those with "knotty joints" The "knotty joints" arrest the impetuousness of the disposition and give reflection, love of detail in all their work and are more frequently found in the hands of all great organisers and those who require thought and reflection in carrying out their plans.

CHAPTER IV

THE NAILS OF THE HAND

A STUDY of the Nails of the Hand is a remarkably accurate guide to many diseases. This part of Palmistry is now recognised by the majority of medical men, who seldom fail quietly to observe the appearance of the nails on a patient's hand.

They are peculiarly indicative of hereditary diseases, especially lungs, heart, nerves, and spine.

They are divided into four very distinct classes. Long, Short, Broad, and Narrow.

LONG NAILS

When the Nails are found very long, the general constitution never appears to be so strong as when they are medium in size.

Persons with long Nails are more liable to all diseases of the Lungs and Chest (Plate V., Part II.), and still more so when these long Nails are seen ribbed or fluted, with the ribs running upward from the base to the edge of the nail.

The same type of Nail, but shorter in appearance, indicates that the delicacy lies higher up towards the throat, and denotes tendencies for laryngitis, inflammation of the throat, and all bronchial troubles.

When especially long Nails are bluish in colour, they denote a still more delicate constitution, coupled with poor circulation of the blood.

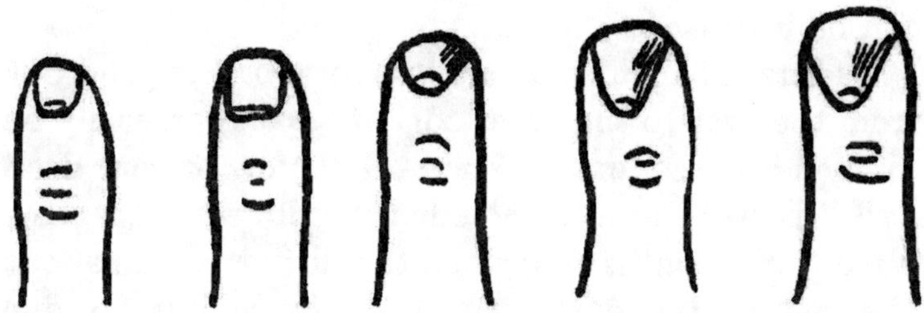

SHORT SQUARE NAILS. WEAK ACTION OF THE HEART.

SHELL-SHAPED NAILS. STRONG TENDENCY TOWARDS PARALYSIS.

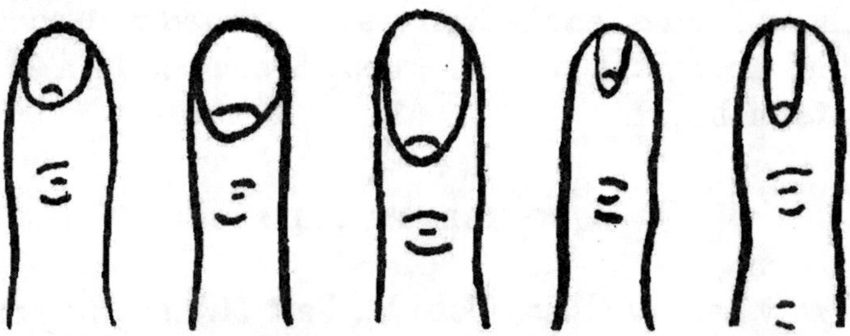

DELICACY OF THROAT.

CHEST DELICATE AND BRONCHIAL.

LUNGS DELICATE.

SPINAL WEAKNESS.

SPINAL WEAKNESS.

PLATE V.—PART II.

SHORT NAILS

Nails short in appearance denote a tendency towards weak action of the heart, more especially so when the "moons" are very small or barely noticeable. When the Nails appear very flat and sunk into the flesh at the base they denote nerve diseases. When they are "ribbed" across the Nail from side to side, the danger is still more apparent.

When a deep furrow is found across the Nail, it is a sign in any hand that an unusual call has recently been made on the nervous system by illness. If the following rule be studied, the date of this illness or strain can be very clearly indicated.

As it takes about nine months for a nail to grow out from the base to the outer edge, the nail can easily be divided into sections. When the furrow or very deep "rib" is seen close to the edge, the illness took place about nine months ago; when the furrow is seen about the centre, the date was about from four to five months, and when at the base, about one month previously.

White spots on the Nails are a sign of general delicacy, and when the Nail is seen covered with small white flecks, the whole nervous system is in a low state of health.

LONG NARROW NAILS

Very narrow Nails (Plate V., Part II.), show spinal weakness, and when extremely curved and very thin they indicate curvature of the spine and great delicacy of the constitution.

FLAT NAILS

When the Nails appear very flat and inclined to lift themselves up from the flesh towards their outer edge, the threatened danger is towards paralysis, and still more so when they look like a shell and are pointed towards the base (Plate V., Part II.). When these

Nails are without any signs of moons, and whitish or bluish in colour, the disease is in a very advanced stage.

THE MOONS OF THE NAILS

Large "Moons" always denote strong action of the heart and rapid circulation of the blood, but when unusually large they indicate too much pressure on the heart, rapidity in its beat, the valves over-strained and danger of bursting some blood vessel in the heart or in the brain.

Small "Moons" indicate the reverse of this; they always denote poor circulation, weak action of the heart and anæmia of the brain.

When close to death the "Moons" are the first to take on a bluish look, and later on the entire Nail becomes blue or almost black in colour.

CHAPTER V

THE MOUNTS OF THE HAND AND THEIR MEANING

THE Mounts of the Hand (Plate VI., Part II.) vary in the most remarkable manner in accordance with the character and dispositions of races and their different temperaments.

In almost all the Southern and more emotional races, these Mounts are more noticeable than those belonging to Northern countries. It has been observed that all people with the Mounts apparent or prominent are more swayed by their feelings and emotions than those people who have flat palms and undeveloped Mounts.

The names given to the Mounts of the Hand are those also given to the seven principal planets that sway the destiny of our earth, viz., the Sun, Moon, Venus, Mercury, Mars, Jupiter, and Saturn.

These names were given to the Mounts by the Greek students of this subject, and were associated by them with the qualities attributed to these seven planets, such as:

Venus = Love, sensuality and passion.
Mars = Vitality, courage, fighting, etc.
Mercury = Mentality, commerce, science.
Moon = Imagination, romance, changeability.
Sun = Brilliancy, fruitfulness, success.
Jupiter = Ambition, power, domination.
Saturn = Reserve, melancholy, seriousness.

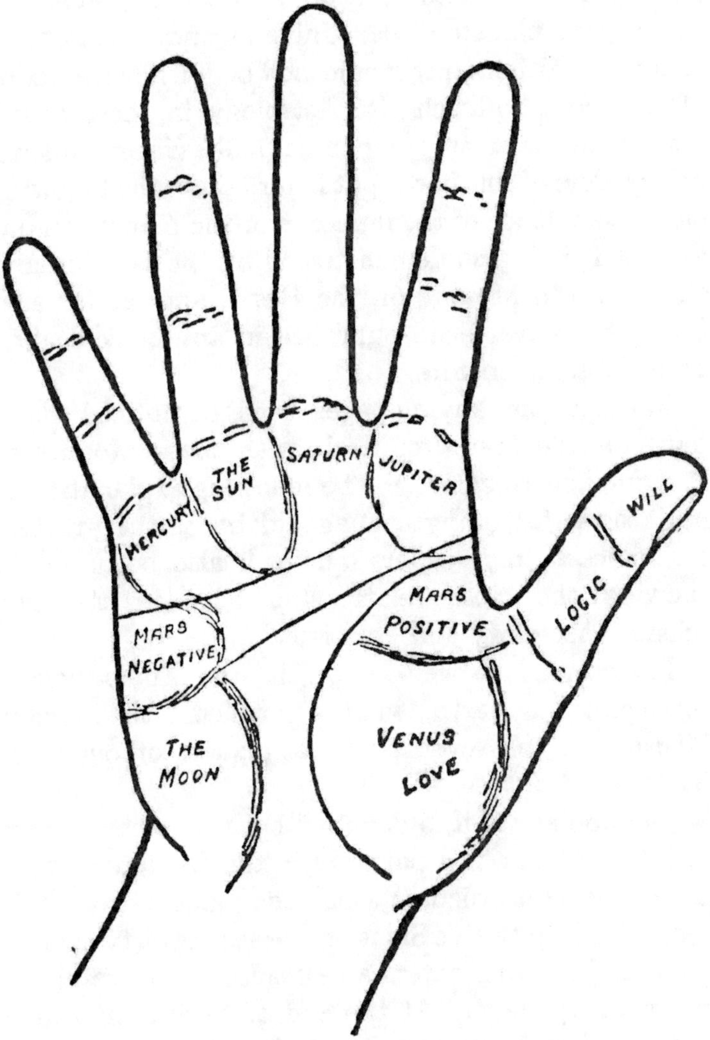

PLATE VI.—PART II.

THE MOUNTS OF THE HAND

In my own long experience I could not help but remark the intimate relation between the effect of these great planets of our Universe and humanity in general. Although it would not be within the scope of this work to teach also Astrology in these pages, I must, however, in order to help all earnest students and readers of this book, put before them the following curious evidence of the influence of the planets on our lives. This is also demonstrated by the position and shape of the Mounts on the Hand, and, as far as I know, has never been published in any book dealing with Palmistry before.

In the accompanying pages it will be noticed that I have for the first time dealt with these Mounts as Positive and Negative. The following explanation of my reason for doing this should be of the greatest assistance to my readers, and will also be useful in showing the close relationship between the two sciences Astrology and Palmistry.

There are, it is well-known, in the Zodiac which surrounds our earth, what are called "the twelve Houses" of the seven principal planets of our Solar System.

The Zodiac itself is decribed both by Astronomers and Astrologers as a pathway in the Universe, about sixteen degrees broad, in which the planets travel. It is divided into twelve Signs or Houses of thirty degrees each, and our Sun enters a new sign on an average of every thirty days. At the end of twelve months it has completed the zodiacal circle of 360 degrees, or one Solar year.

The Sun, the creator of life, and itself the greatest mystery of our Universe, is in bulk 330,000 times larger than our earth. It therefore follows that in entering a new sign of the Zodiac, it changes the magnetic vibrations of the effect of each sign towards our earth. Consequently it is reasonable to presume that a person born, say in April, and another in May, would have very different characteristics and naturally a distinct destiny, because character is Fate or Destiny.

My readers will now easily follow me when I state that, especially as regards health and disease, the following tables concerning the Mounts of the Hand, taken in conjunction with the date of birth, will enable them, when reading the hand, to tell many things with an accuracy that will be most convincing both to themselves and to their hearers.

CHAPTER VI

THE MOUNT OF MARS

THIS Mount has two positions on the palm (Plate VI., Part II.); the first is to be found immediately under the upper part of the Line of Life, and the other opposite to it in the space lying between the Line of Heart and the Line of Head. The first relates to the physical characteristics and the second to the mental.

The first if large is Positive, and it has more importance when the person is born between the dates of March 21st and April 21st, and in a minor way until April 28th, which portion of the year in the Zodiac is called the House of Mars (Positive).

The second is considered Negative, and it has more importance when the person is born between October 21st and November 21st, and in a minor way until November 28th, because in the Zodiac this portion of the year is denoted as the House of Mars (Negative).

We will now consider the difference of these two positions, how distinctly they affect the mind and temperament, and also their relation as to health and tendency towards disease.

THE FIRST MOUNT OF MARS

In the first Mount of Mars, at the commencement of the Line of Life, and especially when the subject is born in the House of Mars (March 21st to April 21st, and in a minor way until the 28th), he possesses a strong martial nature which will make its tendencies manifest in all actions of the life, whether the man be a business man, a soldier, or a leader of men in any line whatever.

These subjects are born fighters in every sense of the word. They brook little or no control in all their affairs; they aspire to be leaders in whatever career they undertake, and with even average intelligence they generally become heads of business houses or organisations and take on large responsibilities.

They have great obstinacy of purpose and determination, they resent all criticism, they are decided and dogmatic in all their views, and seldom ask the advice of others, until it is too late to alter their purpose for good or evil.

They must do everything their own way, and as they always believe their way is the only right one they resent the slightest interference from others, and will even turn on their best friend who may attempt to dissuade them from their plans or purpose.

They can only be handled or managed by kindness, patience, tact, or by their affections.

The slightest attempt to fight or coerce them will bring them up "in arms" in a moment. The temper is hasty and explosive, but at the same time quickly over, and when the storm subsides they bitterly regret the outburst of passion and the cruel things they may have said in the heat of the moment.

As a rule these people are good-natured and generous, but spasmodic and impulsive in all their actions. Their greatest fault lies in their impulsiveness and lack of self-control, and unless a good Line of Head be shown on the hands, they rush madly into all kinds of difficulties and dangers and often make a complete muddle of their opportunities and the magnificent powers of leadership that they nearly all possess.

These people as a rule are unhappy in their love affairs or domestic life. They rarely meet women who understand them, and if they are lucky enough to escape opposition from their wives, they usually meet with it in their children.

In health they are prone to fevers and blood diseases, especially in their early life. In youth they are also very liable to fits, epilepsy, severe headaches, often water on the brain, and suffer greatly with their teeth.

In old age they have a grave liability towards apoplexy, vertigo, pains in the head and softening of the brain, and especially so if on their hands the Line of Head looks frayed, or made up of little pieces like a chain.

Such people should be advised to cultivate repose self-control, and above all to avoid wines, spirits, and stimulants of all kinds, to which as a rule these natures are very much inclined.

They should endeavour to sleep more than any other class, to take more recreation and exercise in the open air, and above all things to curb their pride and control their temper.

The higher types of these subjects and those among them who practise self-restraint, can rise to almost any height in life and do great things for the benefit of their fellow men.

THE SECOND MOUNT OF MARS

The second Mount of Mars, lying between the Heart and Head Line (Plate VI., Part II.), is more important when the subject is born between the dates of 21st October and the 21st November and until November 28th. In the Zodiac this period of the year is called the House of Mars Negative or Mental.

In character they are the complete opposite of the former type, all the Mars qualities being in the mind and in the mental attitude towards people and things.

The latter type are mentally very courageous, and possess *moral courage* more than physical. They hate to have scenes, or to be mixed up with physical violence or bloodshed.

They love to fight mentally, however, and in debates or arguments they also fight to the finish. They are more quietly determined than the former class of Mars subjects. They are even more obstinate in their views, but conceal their opinions, and often pass for assenting parties when in reality they are but waiting for the right opportunity to strike their "mental blow" and confuse their opponent.

These people make better organisers than leaders, and their mental martial spirit often finds a splendid field for their talents as the brain behind an army. In plans, tactics and strategy, in carefully thought-out stores of ammunitions, provisions, or in financial schemes that may bring ruin or discomfiture on a more warlike enemy.

When not highly cultivated or developed, they

employ cunning and craft of every description to carry out their plans. They will stop at nothing to carry out their purpose. They can be the most treacherous and deadly enemies of all, and poison in opposition to the sword is one of the chief weapons they most readily employ.

All these Mars Negative people have a mysterious power of magnetism, which they seem almost unconsciously to use in their dealings with others. They make natural hypnotists and thought-readers, and have strong leanings towards occultism and secret societies of all kinds. When on a highly developed plane, they use these wonderful qualities for the good of others, especially if they take up the study of medicine or science, for which work they seem usually well suited.

Mars Negative people are generally so versatile and many-sided that they are the most difficult of all to place in some special career. If a good Line of Head be found on the hand, then there is nothing in the world of mental endeavour in which they will not make a success. It is a curious fact that these people seldom carry out what they were first trained for, and in fact in the course of their lives they are likely to change their profession or vocation as many times as the proverbial cat has lives.

The worst fault of this type is that they are rather too adaptable to their surroundings and to the people with whom they come in contact. If they are thrown with evil-minded persons they are inclined to adapt themselves to their companions and even attempt to "go one better," but if in contact with good influences they just as rapidly develop the best that is in them.

Their period of the Zodiac has from time immemorial been symbolised in their lower development as the figure of a scorpion wounding its own tail, and in their higher development that of an eagle with its head pointing upwards to the sky.

Such symbols perfectly illustrate the dual nature of the type under consideration. In their lower aspect no type can be more vicious or harmful, even to wounding themselves and bringing about their own destruction. In their higher form, however, there is probably no class whose spiritual nature can, like the eagle, soar to such heights or be so free from earthly ties.

Mars Negative people, especially when young, should above all things be carefully brought up with good companions. They should be especially warned to control their sex nature and be kept aloof from all perverse persons and evil books.

As regards health, this type is usually inclined to be both slight and delicate in their early years, but generally incline towards corpulency after passing middle life. Both the men and women have a likelihood of weakness or illness in the sex organs, especially in youth, also in the kidneys and the bladder, while in advanced years the stomach and digestive organs become disordered. All through their lives they should be most careful and abstemious in their diet.

CHAPTER VII

THE MOUNT OF JUPITER AND ITS MEANING

THE Mount of Jupiter is found at the base of the first finger (Plate VI., Part II.). When large, it shows desire to dominate, to rule and command others, to lead and organise, and to carry out some distinct object. But these good qualities will only be employed if the Line of Head is clear and long. When this line is poor and badly formed, then a large Mount of Jupiter gives pride, excess of vanity, a self-confident and a self-opinionated person. But on what is known as a good well-marked hand, there is no Mount more excellent and no surer indication of success from sheer strength of character and purpose.

This Mount may be considered Positive when a person is found born between November 21st and December 20th, and in a minor way until the 28th. These persons are naturally ambitious, fearless and determined in all they undertake, but in acting on their impulses, they generally "hit too straight from the shoulder," or show their ambition too plainly, and so arouse antagonism, opposition, and enmity.

They concentrate all their attention on whatever they may be doing at the moment and see no way but their own, especially if they feel the least opposition to their plans. They are, however, honourable and high principled in almost all they undertake and respond to any trust or confidence placed in them.

They are usually extremely truthful and bitterly resent any attempt at deception, and do not hesitate to unmask any effort to deceive others, even when such an action on their part may ruin their own plans.

They have great enterprise in business and all matters requiring organisation, and easily become the heads of businesses, or hold responsible positions in government offices or under the government. They rarely become politicians, for the simple reason that they cannot bear to bend to any party plans or schemes.

They are perhaps the most independent of all types in choosing their own careers. Because their father may have happened to be a clergyman will be no reason for them to follow his example or even hold the same views on religion.

It is for this reason that in early life such subjects are a cause of worry and anxiety to their parents; but they should always be allowed to choose their own career and even change it a dozen times if they wish, until at last they find their true vocation.

The great fault of this class is that they are inclined to go to extremes in all things, and in doing so exhaust their efforts, and then change and fly off in another direction. But in all cases where the Line of Head is well-marked, especially when lying straight across the palm, there is no height in position or responsibility that they may not reach.

HEALTH

These subjects are more inclined to suffer with rheumatism and acid complaints than from any other form of disease, also inflammation of the tongue and throat, boils, carbuncles, eczema, and all skin troubles.

THE MOUNT OF JUPITER (NEGATIVE)

The Mount of Jupiter may be considered negative or mental when the subject is born between the dates of February 19th and March 20th, and in a slighter degree until the 28th.

In this case the ambition takes rather the mental form than what might be termed material. Brain work and brain development is more their speciality than other forms of effort.

They seem to possess a kind of natural understanding of things and easily acquire all sorts of knowledge about a large variety of things, especially the history of countries, races, peoples, geographical, botanical, and geological researches.

In spite of this mental ambition, these people are usually so very sensitive and so lacking in self-confidence that they find the greatest difficulty in carrying out their plans and making people believe in their projects. For this reason they appear to shrink from coming before the public, and have to stand aside and see others getting the credit for what really was their plan.

A great number of literary people, composers and artists are born in this period and exhibit all the qualities that it represents. It is again a strong clear Line of Head which, if found on the hand, will determine whether the mental will power is sufficient to make this type overcome its natural sensitiveness and use the great qualities they have to carry out their aims and ambitions.

HEALTH

People born in this period suffer largely from despondency, insomnia, and a feeling of martyrdom. Like the Positive type of the same Mount, they are also much inclined towards rheumatism and disorders brought on through the blood.

They also suffer from internal chills, liver, and very often jaundice. Climate has the greatest possible effect upon their health, so they should endeavour to live in a bright, dry atmosphere and have plenty of air and exercise, and variety of change and travel.

CHAPTER VIII

THE MOUNT OF SATURN AND ITS MEANING

THE Mount of Saturn is found at the base of the second finger (*see* Plate VI., Part II.). Its chief characteristics are love of solitude, prudence, quiet determination, the study of serious sombre things, the belief in fatalism and in the ultimate destiny of all things.

A complete absence of this Mount indicates a more or less frivolous way of looking at life, while an exaggeration of it denotes an exaggeration of all the qualities it represents.

The Mount of Saturn may be considered Positive when the subject is found to be born between the following dates, December 21st and January 20th, and during the subsequent seven days while this period is fading out and being overlapped by the period following.

People born in these dates have strong will force and mentality, but they usually feel exceptionally lonely and isolated in going through life.

They are very much children of fate and circumstances, over which they appear to have no control, and seem to make or mar their careers independently of their strong will.

In character they are usually remarkable for their

independence of thought and action, they also detest being under the restraint of others.

For kindness and sympathy they will do almost anything, but they usually feel so isolated that they scarcely believe in the affections that may be offered.

They have strange ideas of love and duty, and for this reason they are usually called somewhat peculiar by those few who attempt to penetrate their isolation.

They have a deeply devotional nature, even when appearing not to be religious, and they make every effort to do good, especially to the masses, even when there may be no likelihood of their getting recognition or reward for their efforts.

Such people as a rule feel the responsibilities of life too heavily and in consequence often become despondent and gloomy or retire into their own shell.

If at all inclined to be very religious, they generally go to extremes and become fanatical in any Church they may adopt.

Mysticism and occultism of all kinds appeal very strongly to their inner nature, but here again they are also inclined to go to extremes.

They almost worship clever, intellectual people, and are deep thinkers in all matters that interest them, but they cannot brook interference in their views from others.

They are often found holding positions of great responsibility, but in all matters fatalism seems to play a strange rôle in their life. They seem chosen to be the instrument or mouthpiece of Destiny, often hurling thousands to destruction in what they believe is their duty. If called upon to make a sacrifice of their own flesh and kin they will be the first to plunge the knife into the heart of their dearest.

Nearly all people born in this period are strange, strong characters, equally feared, loved, and hated.

HEALTH

The chief tendencies towards illness with persons born in this period are towards rheumatism, gout, pains and swellings in the feet and legs, also accidents to the feet, knees, and limbs, trouble with the liver and kidneys, ruptures, and disease of the teeth and ears.

THE MOUNT OF SATURN (NEGATIVE)

The Mount of Saturn may be considered negative or mental when the person is found born between the dates of January 21st and February 18th, and also for the seven days following.

These people are like the preceding type in almost all things, except that the same things appear to affect them more mentally than physically.

They also feel lonely in life, but more mentally than the former type—they seem to feel less companionship in their ideas and thoughts, whereas the former feel it more in their lives and careers.

These latter types are more sensitive and very easily wounded in their feelings.

They read character instinctively and seem to "see through" people too easily to be really happy. They bitterly resent being taken in or deceived, and when they think they have been, they astonish people by the bitterness of their resentment.

They make loyal, true friends, if their feelings are once aroused, and they will undergo any sacrifice for the sake of a friend, but they will stop at nothing to avenge an injury if they think they have been deceived.

They are usually very active for the public good, and they give a good deal of their time and money to doing good, but in their own way. Like the positive type of Saturn they have very decided views of their own about religion and especially the regular observances and ceremonials of Church life.

They are very different from the previous type in that they usually take a keen interest in public meetings and large gatherings of people. They love theatres, concerts, and places of amusement, and yet always if they told the truth, they feel alone in life.

They have a quiet controlling power with their eyes, and although highly nervous people themselves, yet they have the greatest control over excitable and nervous patients and also over the insane. It is a strange fact that in the run of their careers they seem fated to be brought into contact with such cases.

HEALTH

These people suffer most from the nerves of the stomach and the digestive organs, and ordinary remedies seem to fail entirely to relieve them.

They have as a rule poor circulation of the blood, cold feet and hands, very delicate teeth, and suffer much from accidents and hurts to the feet, ankles and limbs.

They seldom feel strong in health and yet they have enormous power of resistance, and when a call is made on their will power, they usually astonish every one by what they can stand, especially if they in any way think that their duty or principles are involved or at stake.

CHAPTER IX

THE MOUNT OF THE SUN AND ITS MEANING

THE Mount of the Sun is found under the base of the third finger. To this Mount the Greeks also gave the name of Mount of Apollo (Plate (VI., Part II.).

When large or well developed it indicates glory, publicity, a desire to shine before one's fellows. It is always considered a good Mount to have large.

It also indicates enthusiasm for the beautiful in all things, whether one follows an artistic calling or not. People with this Mount large, even if they have success in practical life, build beautiful houses or have artistic surroundings of some sort. They also have an expansive temperament, are generous and luxurious in all their tastes. They are bright and sunny by nature and have a forceful, happy, lucky personality.

This Mount may be considered Positive when the subject is found to be born between the dates of July 21st and August 20th, and generally until the 28th of this month, which portion of the Zodiac is called the "House of the Sun."

These people represent what may be called the heart force of the human race, and as a rule are generous and sympathetic even to an extreme.

They have great force of character and personality,

and even when constrained by circumstances to exist in the lower walks of life, they play, even there, a rôle distinct from their fellows, and their clean-cut, well-marked personality is sure to make itself manifest.

At heart they are really most sympathetic, though they often seem to hide this quality on account of their strong sense of trying to force people to do what is right towards others.

They have no mercy for "weaklings" or evaders of the truth, and in brutal frankness they will even denounce their own children should they find them falling into evil ways.

They display the greatest loyalty if any friend of theirs is attacked, especially if in an underhand way. They love intensely and they hate intensely. Theirs is no middle path, for they must be either at one extreme or the other.

Although truthful and naturally honest they often get terribly deceived, and the danger is with such people that towards the sunset of their lives, the glorious Sun that has shone, as it were, through them gets darkened by the deceit and treachery of others and sets in clouds, or gets hidden before the ending of life's pathway comes to view.

Many of these people who have cheered others, who have brought their grand sunshine of good into the hearts of others, cannot cheer themselves when the twilight comes, and so they often fall victims to gloom and melancholy, and many commit suicide.

Among other marked characteristics these people are extremely proud and would sooner die than ask favours from others. They are extremely easily wounded through their pride and are unusually sensitive.

Impetuous and hot-tempered, they make many enemies, and when engaged in public life, which they are usually well fitted for, they often find themselves bitterly attacked in the most unscrupulous manner.

HEALTH

Those born in the dates I have given, or who have the Mount of the Sun large, are most inclined to suffer with pains, palpitations, and trouble of the heart, head, and ears; with inflammation of the eyes, kidneys, and swellings and injuries to the feet.

MOUNT OF THE SUN (NEGATIVE)

This Mount may be considered Negative when the subject is found born between January 21st and February 18th, and for the seven days following.

In this case they are far more successful when managing for others than for themselves.

They are usually found most active in their plans towards the relief of all distress and for what they believe to be the public good.

They are also often as a class found in governmental positions, or as leaders of some party or section of public opinion. Usually they take the part of the "under dog," and cause themselves to be greatly abused and disliked by the richer and more powerful classes.

They seldom attract wealth as do those of the Positive type, who are usually lucky in money, and when they do they are inclined to impoverish themselves in their efforts to help those around them, or in the execution of their philanthropic plans for the good of the poorer classes.

In strange apparent contradiction to this, these people are usually excellent in business and in their financial plans, but again it is more for others than for themselves. Many of them make fortunes for others and keep the merest pittance for their own homes.

As a rule, they find great pleasure in public ceremonies, and meetings of all kinds. They love theatres and all places where large numbers of people congregate, and when wound up to the occasion they can display great eloquence, power of argument, and influence in debates. They rarely hold the positions they win for the run of their careers, they seem to play the rôle of the moment, and when that is passed they just as quickly retire into obscurity or into a quiet private life, and often end their days in the most unusual or unheard-of places.

Quite the reverse of the Positive type, these people seldom if ever commit suicide; on the contrary, they can endure any kind of martyrdom or suffering. They are buoyed up with the feeling they have done their duty to their fellow beings, and this feeling seems to sustain them against all disappointments, or losses or attacks on their name.

HEALTH

These children of the Negative period of the Sun suffer mostly with the stomach and internal organs, also with poor circulation of blood, loss of natural heat, and with liver and kidney complaints.

They are also prone to have accidents to their bones, especially to limbs, knees, and ankles.

Very dry climates and plenty of sunlight is their greatest safeguard against all their maladies.

CHAPTER X

THE MOUNT OF MERCURY AND ITS MEANING

THE Mount of Mercury is found under the base of the fourth finger (Plate VI., Part II.). On a good hand it is a favourable Mount to have, but on a hand shewing evil tendencies, especially mental, it increases the bad indications.

It seems to relate more to the mind than anything else. It gives quickness of brain, wit, thought, eloquence. It also relates to adaptability in science and commerce, but if evilly afflicted, it denotes mental excitability, nervousness, lack of concentration, trickiness in business, and everything that is unreliable in character.

This Mount should always be considered with the kind of Line of Head found on the hand.

With a Line of Head long and well marked, it increases all the promise of mental aptitude and success, but with a weak, badly marked, or irregular Head Line, it augments all its weak or bad indications.

THE MOUNT OF MERCURY (POSITIVE)

This Mount can be considered positive when the subject is found to be born between the dates of May 21st and June 20th, and until the 27th of that month, but during the last seven days its influence is considered dying out and not so strong.

People born in this period are represented in the Zodiac by the symbolism of the twins. It is a curious fact that all persons born in this part of the year are singularly dual in character and temperament. One side of their nature may, in fact, be described as perpetually pulling against the other, and although nearly always possessed with unusual intelligence, they often spoil their lives by lack of continuity in their plans and in their purpose.

They seldom seem to have a fixed idea of what they really want. They change their plans or their occupations at a moment's notice, and unless they chance to be very happily married, they are just as uncertain in marriage.

They are the most difficult of all classes to understand. In temperament they are hot and cold in the same moment, they may love passionately with one side of their nature and just as quickly dislike with the other.

They are very critical, and especially notice small faults or mannerisms in others, and they can express their views with a sarcasm that is as cutting as it is clever.

In all business dealings or affairs where a subtle, keen mentality is useful, they can out-distance all rivals, provided they are sufficiently interested to enter into the competition.

They are excellent in diplomacy and are gifted talkers, but they usually leave their listeners at the end of their conversation no wiser than they were at the beginning.

If taken as they are and with their moods, they are the most delightful people imaginable, but one must never expect them to be the same to-day that they were yesterday.

They believe that they are the most truthful persons in the world, and so they may be at the moment they are telling the story, but to them moments seem entire lives, and so in a day or a week the same story may have a totally different colouring.

None of these people will probably admit this to be true of his character, but a little study will convince anyone that it is a fairly accurate description of this subject's chief characteristics.

Mental work, especially the class of mental work that requires quickness of wit and change, appeals to them more than any other. They make clever actors, barristers, and a certain class of public speakers, also diplomatists, stock brokers, company promoters, or inventors of new methods in business. In all careers that require keenness of brain, they can attain success, provided they have developed a sufficient amount of will power and continuity of purpose to stick long enough to any one thing.

HEALTH

Everything that can affect the nerves and the nervous system especially, afflicts these people.

Indigestion caused by nervous worry or anxiety, catalepsy, paralysis, afflictions of the tongue, stammering, insomnia, vivid dreams; to all such things they are specially liable. They are also inclined towards delicacy of the throat and bronchial tubes, and particularly to trouble with the nose and eyes.

THE MOUNT OF MERCURY (NEGATIVE)

This Mount may be considered negative when the persons are born between August 21st and September

20th, and until the 27th, but these last seven days of this period are not so marked, but take more from the characteristics of the incoming sign.

People belonging to this negative type of the Mount of Mercury have all the good points of the positive class, and even some added in their favour. For example, they stick longer and with more continuity to whatever study or career they adopt. They have hardly the quickness or the brilliancy of the first type, but they have a more solid, plodding course of action, and as a general rule they make more out of their lives.

They are also more materialistic and practical in their views of life, but they analyse and reason everything from their own way of thinking outwards towards others. If they see a thing is right, it is right to them, and for this reason they are often found doing exactly the opposite from what one would expect.

Women born in this period are especially curious puzzles. They are either extremely virtuous or the direct opposite, either extremely truthful and conventional or the reverse; but whether good or bad, they are all a law unto themselves, and in all things they usually think of themselves first.

People born in this period often abandon their husbands or their children just because they think they ought to do so. They also are liable to change their religious views half way through life, or from the most conventional suddenly become the reverse. In the same way women who have commenced their career by leading unconventional lives, may just as suddenly become religious and enter some extremely severe order or community.

Again, as in the positive type, it is the Line of Head

that must be carefully considered if one should endeavour to form an estimate of what they will eventually become.

If it be clear and straight, their best qualities will, as a rule, come to their rescue; but if weak or poorly marked, it is more than likely, especially with this class, that the evil side of the nature will in the end predominate.

HEALTH

These people are more open to mental suggestion as far as health is concerned than any other class.

If they think they are ill it is quite sufficient that they are so, and they can become cured in exactly the same manner.

In reality they have excellent constitutions, except when they are ruined by taking drugs and medicines.

As they always imagine that they have something the matter, they are invariably the willing prey of quack doctors and every new cure that is advertised.

They can hardly pass a chemist's shop without buying something, and if they sit next to a doctor at a dinner table, they are certain to walk off with some prescription.

Their greatest fault is that they will persist in talking to everyone of their supposed ailments or afflictions, for the slightest ache, pain, or anything that concerns them, has the most exaggerated importance in their mind.

On the contrary, Nature can do more for these people than for any other class of humanity. Peace of mind, a country life, and plenty of fresh air will banish all their ills and ailments into oblivion.

But, if badly mated, or living in unhappy surroundings, their health quickly breaks up, and if they cannot make a change into happier conditions, then no medicine in all the world can help them.

CHAPTER XI

THE MOUNT OF THE MOON AND ITS MEANING

THE Mount of the Moon, or as it is also called the Mount of Luna, is found on the base of the hand under the end of the Line of Head (Plate VI., Part II.).

This Mount relates to everything that has to do with the imaginative faculties, the emotional artistic temperament, romance, ideality, poetry, change of scenery, travel, and such like.

This Mount may be considered positive when it looks high or well-developed, and also when the subject is found to be born between the dates of June 21st and July 20th, and until July 27th.

People who belong to this positive class are gifted with strong imagination which tinges everything they do or say. They are intensely romantic, but idealistic in their desires, and have not that passionate or sensual nature that is given by the Mount of Venus on the opposite side of the palm.

As a rule they have the inventive faculties well developed, and succeed in inventions and in all new ideas in whatever careers they may have entered.

Even business people born in this period are remarkable for their originality, and the inventive manner in which they will tackle the most practical affair.

They are, however, inclined to speculate or gamble even with their chances, also in stocks, business or, in fact, anything in which they are engaged.

Although their imagination is large, they often achieve great success and make money in business. Some great financiers and heads of large organisations have been born in this period and have also had the Mount of Luna very highly developed on their hands.

It has been said "that what one sees in one's dreams one shall gain in reality," but the fact remains that imaginative people have been found among the most successful of all classes. Imagination may be another name for Inspiration.

People born in this period are seldom hide-bound by any rule of thumb or set convention. They love what is new in everything, and perhaps for this reason they love travel and change, and generally see the greater part of this planet before they voyage over the last river of all.

Change in every way affects their careers as it also does their lives. Even the successful members of this period have more ups and downs than almost any other class.

They rarely, however, give in to the blows of Fate. Their imagination probably helps them through, and they seldom remain down or down-hearted for long.

Inventors, a large number of artists, musicians, and composers are found among people of this type, but almost without exception they have a love of mystic and occult things, and their dreams and visions are tangible and clear.

These Children of the Moon owe much to the influence of their planet that they are even more magnetic and successful when the Moon appears in the heavens.

Even their health appears to change and become better under her benign influence, and they should always be advised to commence their plans or operations when their planet is to be seen illuminating the skies.

That the Moon plays an important rôle in the affairs of this earth cannot for a moment be doubted. Recent discoveries are every day revealing more and more that her strange magnetic influence has a power almost beyond belief in its effect upon the growth of vegetables, and even inanimate things.

There are other thinkers besides those interested in occult subjects who have noticed the effect of this planet on mundane things. If the Moon can affect vegetables, eggs, and the growth of chickens, as it is proved to do, how much more easily and wonderfully it must affect the grey matter of the human brain, which is the most subtle and mysterious essence of all.

People born in the period I have mentioned should be most careful of those with whom they associate, because they are extraordinarily sensitive to the magnetism of others.

They should, if possible, avoid marrying early in life unless they are absolutely sure they have met their affinity. These natures both change and develop rapidly, and they have a strong tendency to "grow away" from those with whom they associate in early life. It is the same with partners in business; they should be as much as possible "on their own" or, if partnerships are made, they should not be of a binding or restricting order, and provision should always be made for the partnership to be dissolved when it has become irksome.

HEALTH

These Children of the Moon are chiefly inclined towards all watery ailments and inflammatory diseases. In early life they are prone towards having water on the brain, gastric and dysentery attacks, and later in life, inflammation of the lungs and chest, pleurisy, and dropsy.

THE MOUNT OF THE MOON (NEGATIVE)

This Mount is considered negative when it appears very flat on the hand, and it may also be taken as negative when people are found to be born between the dates of January 21st and February 20th, and in a minor degree, until about February 27th.

People born between these dates have good mental powers, but their imaginative faculties are seldom as much in evidence as is so strongly the case with the positive period.

These persons, on the contrary, are good and quiet reasoners-out of problems and matters relating to the organisation of business, and are also excellent in all forms of government work. They make splendid heads of departments and rise to any responsibility very quickly and easily.

They are high-minded and have very decided views on love, duty, and social life. They make great efforts to do good to others, but as a rule their best work is done towards helping the masses more than individuals.

They are extremely kind-hearted and love to give a helping hand when they can, but at the same time they have an unfortunate knack of making many bitter enemies, and when holding government positions they are most bitterly attacked by the opposition press.

Their work seldom receives its proper recognition and reward until they have passed from their sphere of influence, or have left this world of mistrust and ingratitude.

They generally make excellent speakers, but more from "plain speaking," in a particular way of their own.

As a rule they espouse the unpopular cause and take the part of the under dog in the fight.

They make devoted and loyal friends once their friendship is aroused, but at the same time they are extremely sensitive and easily wounded by those they care for.

They are strongly inclined to be religious and generally bring their religious views into all they do. They are in danger of becoming too fanatical, and when opposed, they become extremely obstinate, dogmatic, and hard to manage.

Heavy responsibility for others suits them best of all, especially if such responsibility lies in the form of government work, or in some position of management.

HEALTH

These people usually worry themselves into bad health. They overwork themselves and bring on nervous breakdowns, palpitation and weakness of the heart, and often paralysis. They suffer with the nerves of the stomach, acidity of the blood, rheumatism, liver complaints, and gout. They are particularly liable to meet with accidents to the feet, ankles, and limbs.

They should be very guarded when travelling by water, for they seldom get through life without sooner or later experiencing grave danger of drowning.

CHAPTER XII

THE MOUNT OF VENUS AND ITS MEANING

THE portion of the palm under the base of the Thumb and inside the Line of Life is called the Mount of Venus (Plate VI., Part II.). When well-formed and not too large, it denotes a desire for love and companionship, the desire to please, worship of beauty in every form, the artistic and emotional temperament, and it is usually very prominent in the hands of all artists, singers, and musicians.

This Mount, the science of Physiology teaches, covers one of the most important blood vessels in the palm, viz., the "Great Palmer Arch." If this loop or arch is large, it indicates a plentiful supply of blood and strong active circulation; consequently, the health is more robust. It is found that persons possessing this Mount well developed, being in active strong health, are naturally more full of passion than those individuals in poor health, and who, in consequence, have this portion of the hand either flat or poorly developed. Hence, when this Mount is large it has been considered to show passion and larger sensuality than when flat, flabby, or non-developed.

This Mount is therefore called Positive when high or large, and Negative when small or flat.

With the rest of the hand normal, this Mount well shaped is an excellent sign to have, as it denotes magnetism and attraction of one sex to the other, but if found together with vicious or abnormal signs in the hand, it increases those tendencies.

When considered with the birth date, as alluded to in the former chapters, it helps to throw considerable light on characteristics that might otherwise be overlooked.

The student may consider it Positive when the subject is born between April 20th and May 20th, and in a minor way until May 27th, the chief characteristics of this period being as follows:

These persons have a curious dominating power over others, and are found rather inclined to be too dogmatic in their opinions, and also often too unyielding and tyrannical. They are considered stiff-necked and obstinate, but the strange thing is that when they love they become the most abject slaves of all to the object of their devotion, and they will consider no sacrifice too great for that one being who holds or attracts their affection.

They are hospitable and generous, and especially love to entertain their friends. They make wonderfully good hosts, have great taste about food, and love to give excellent dinners.

They dress with great taste, and are generally considered richer than they really are, and they can make a good show on very little.

They are impulsive in their likes and dislikes, rather too frank and outspoken, quick in temper, and when their blood is up they have no restraint on what they say.

Their passion or temper is, however, quickly over,

and when the storm is passed they are most regretful for the wounds their temper may have caused.

These types are most easily influenced by their surroundings, and become morbid and depressed when they are forced to live in gloomy and uncongenial conditions.

Neither the man nor woman born in this period should marry early, for their first attempt is usually a mistake. They are so independent in character that, especially if they marry early and find their mistake, they lead unconventional lives and get severely criticised in consequence.

They are inclined to be very jealous when their affections are roused, especially if the peace of the home is in any way disturbed.

HEALTH

People born in this period have usually short or round-shaped nails which indicate a tendency to suffer with complaints of the throat and nose.[1] They also suffer, as a rule, with pains in the head and ears, swellings in the neck, and have a tendency towards tumours, appendicitis, and other internal troubles, chiefly relating to the intestines.

THE MOUNT OF VENUS (NEGATIVE)

This Mount may be considered Negative when the subject is born between the dates of September 21st and October 20th, and in a minor way until October 27th, and with people born in this period it is seldom found so prominent. The fact is, that the affections these

[1] *See* Chapter on Nails, page 136.

subjects possess may be just as intense, but more mental than physical.

Their love is spiritual rather than sensual, and they crave more for soul companionship than for that of the physical senses.

Of course there are exceptions to all rules, but these exceptions can be easily seen by watching if the Mount of Venus is large with people born in this period.

All mental characteristics rule, however, very strongly. Those born in this latter period have keen intuition and a mental balance of all things not given to the other class. They have presentiments and psychic experiences, dreams, clairvoyance, and such like, which they often spoil by their reasoning faculties, and they endeavour to answer all problems through the medium of their mind or mental faculties.

In love they are nearly always unhappy. They cannot "let themselves go," like the Positive Venus type. They hesitate and miss their opportunities whilst they think or reason, and so love goes by and often leaves them nothing but regret. They should be advised to act more on their first impressions and intuition, and take the opportunities that Fate throws in their way.

They occupy themselves very much with all mental questions concerning their fellow beings. They are often found studying Law, but more with the desire of improving it for others than for their own personal advantage.

They have a great desire for knowledge, and often spend their lives in studying abstruse subjects, but always weighing and balancing each point in the most conscientious manner. They make excellent doctors, judges, lawyers, but more as masters of some particular branch than that of gaining worldly advantage.

HEALTH

The people born in this period are inclined to suffer from lack of physical strength, exhaustion of the nerves, depression of spirits, melancholia, intense feeling of loneliness, and such like. Also severe headaches, pains in the back, loins, and kidneys; just as in the case of those of the other period of this Venus sign they have a great tendency, especially the women, to suffer from internal ailments, and often undergo severe operations.

CHAPTER XIII

ADVICE TO THE STUDENT. THE BEST MEANS TO MAKE CASTS OR TAKE IMPRESSIONS OF THE HANDS

I WOULD strongly advise students of this subject to make casts of hands in plaster of Paris, wax, or any other suitable material, in order to make a library or collection, both for their own private study, and also as a valuable record of their work.

Before I read any hands professionally, I had some thousands of casts, impressions on paper, and photographs of hands in my possession, and I found that I derived the most valuable aid from being able to analyse and study their shapes and markings at my leisure.

In making casts I would advise the very finest plaster of Paris to be used. When the plaster is worked up to the proper consistency, it is necessary to rub a fine oil into the hand before bringing it into contact with the plaster, as otherwise the hair may stick and so cause trouble and annoyance.

Dental wax heated in hot water and made very soft is also an excellent material to make moulds from, especially as it does not make a mess, and is very little trouble to employ.

The great disadvantage of making a collection of casts arises from the large space that such a collection will eventually occupy. To avoid this the student can also make a library of impressions of hands on paper, and keep them marked and numbered in a series of albums or scrap-books that may easily be obtained at any stationer's.

The best means of taking these impressions is to obtain a small gelatine roller used by printers for fine work, such as die stamping, a tube of printer's ink, and a small sheet of glass to roll the ink out until it covers the surface of the roller in an even way.

The roller may then be passed over the surface of the palm, the hand pressed firmly down on a smooth sheet of white paper, and with a little practice, most excellent impressions can easily be obtained.

When the impression is dry it can be dated, numbered, and placed in an album for reference.

In order to remove the black ink from the hand, powdered washing soap, well brushed into the hand with a nail brush, and a little hot water is all that will be found necessary.

These impressions taken with printer's ink are far better than those taken by smoking a sheet of paper by camphor, or by a candle, or any other means.

The best time for examining hands is during the day, first because the light is better and, above all, because the circulation of the blood does not redden the entire palm as it does at night, and the finer lines can consequently easily be detected.

As I described earlier in these pages, the right and left hands should be examined together to note what difference there may be in the shape and position of the lines, but the markings on the right hand are the only ones to be relied on.

Lastly, do not be for ever on the lookout for faults

and failings in the subject whose hands you may be examining, remember no one is perfect, and that faults and failings may in the end be as stepping stones "by which we rise from our dead selves to higher things."

A Selection from the Catalogue of

G. P. PUTNAM'S SONS

Complete Catalogue sent on application

Published by

Facsimile Publisher
Ashok Vihar, Delhi-110052 (India)
Website: www.facsimilepublisher.com

Distributed by

Gyan Books Pvt. Ltd.
5, Ansari Road, Daryaganj, New Delhi-110002 (India)
E-mail: books@gyanbooks.com, Website: www.gyanbooks.com